Go Codeabout

with

C++

Dr. Bharat B. Aggarwal

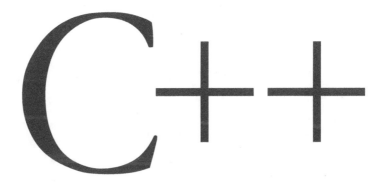

ajc Amar Jefferson Consulting
http://amarjefferson.com

ISBN-13: 978-1507837795
ISBN-10: 1507837798

First Print Edition (March 2015)
Printed by CreateSpace, An Amazon.com Company.
Available from Amazon.com, CreateSpace.com, and other retail outlets.

This edition published by Amar Jefferson Consulting (http://amarjefferson.com)

About the Author

Dr. Bharat B. Aggarwal first started programming in 1975 on an IBM mainframe at IIT Kanpur. After getting his PhD in Mechanical Engineering from University of Massachusetts, Amherst, he worked in fields of engineering R&D and technical software development in the USA and India.

He has programmed in many programming languages including Assembly Language (Intel and DEC), BASIC, LISP, Smalltalk, Prolog, FORTRAN, C, C++, Java and C#. His development experience includes web programming, business software, engineering software and real-time control software. He has taught programming courses for college students and working professionals.

His primary focus is on encouraging the use of programming as tool to promote creativity and to solve everyday problems.

This book is dedicated to my wife Tejinder Jit Aggarwal and my son Amar Jefferson Aggarwal. This book would not have been possible without their participation and support.

Foreword

We have all heard of the Australian term *go walkabout*:

A temporary return to traditional Aboriginal life, taken especially between periods of work or residence in modern society and usually involving a long walking journey on land that is far from towns and cities.

In this book you will go *Codeabout*: a journey of discovery in Codeland, a magical place far from our everyday surroundings. In this enchanted land you will C a magnificent Ruby guarded by a mighty Python who will make you Lisp in fear! You can listen to Basic musical notes like C# while enjoying a cup of Java or making Smalltalk. All that and much more just waiting for you with only one purpose: to let you create worlds of your own imagining where things work the way you want them to! All it takes is curiosity, a sense of wonder and the drive to give life to the worlds of your imagination.

It took God six days to make the world we live in. It will take you a little longer to create your own! But as Lao-Tzu said: "The journey of a thousand miles begins with a single step." Let us begin our journey. With C++.

Table of Contents

Preface

My first experience with programming was in engineering college on an IBM mainframe using punch cards for input. Our teacher insisted that we learn programming using low level machine instructions. A simple program to sort ten numbers became a huge stack of cards full of instructions to move numbers around in memory. We hated it then but it gave us an understanding of how computers worked and how precise and complete the instructions had to be for a program to work. When we learned FORTRAN later in the course, it was a breeze and the programs we wrote were generally error free as the habit of paying attention to details had become ingrained. Our teacher did not get into all the details of the language but taught us the basics and laid a foundation for us to learn more on our own. The objective of this book is to teach the basics of object-oriented programming using C++ to get the readers started on programming and lay the foundation for them to learn more on their own.

> "And how will you inquire into a thing when
> you are wholly ignorant of what it is?"
> From Plato's Dialogue Meno

Over the years, I have read many books and technical articles on software development and programming languages, incorporating the ideas that I liked into my work. This book is based on notes I made as I learned new languages and techniques. The notes came together while teaching a course on C++ programming for first year engineering students in an undergraduate college. Recently, my son saw a printed copy of the notes and insisted I publish them. This book is the result of his push.

This book is not intended to be a comprehensive reference on C++ or to cover all aspects of C++ programming. There are plenty of good comprehensive tomes on C++ written by authors a lot more learned than I am. This book is focused completely on using programming as a tool to solve problems. I have avoided discussions of esoteric details of features of C++ and focused instead on how to use them. The detailed discussions are essential for computer scientists but I do not think we need to burden users of a programming language with them just as we are not burdened with detailed linguistic studies when we learn our native language. We need to demystify programming so that it becomes a natural part of our repertoire just like our native language. Programming is a powerful tool that all of us can use to bring our ideas to life in a dynamic way. It is time to end the view of programming as an arcane world accessible only to geeks!

Acknowledgements

I have learned much from the books, magazines and technical journals I have read over the years. I have also had the good fortune to work with and learn from many talented colleagues. I have incorporated what I have learned from my reading, my colleagues and my own experience in this book. I would like to thank all those who have contributed to my growth and made it possible for me to write this book.

I have listed some of the C++ books I liked in the bibliography. A few of the books are old but still very good for learning the basics.

Source Code

Source code for all examples was tested using Microsoft Visual Studio 2013, Community Edition. The source code can be downloaded from http://amarjefferson.com/codeabout/cpp.

Part

Basics

1 The First Step

Let us begin with a program that prints the message "Hello World!" on the screen:

```
// Hello World!

// header files required by the program
#include <cstdlib>
#include <iostream>

// the main function
int main(void)
{
    std::cout << "Hello World!" << std::endl;
    return EXIT_SUCCESS;
}
```

The program uses several features of C++: a *preprocessor directive* (#include), *header files* (cstdlib and iostream), an *object* (std::cout), *a manipulator* (std::endl), an *operator* (<<), a *constant* (EXIT_SUCCESS), a *keyword* (void), *statements*, *comments* and a *function*. We will look at some of these features briefly in this chapter. We will learn more about them in subsequent chapters.

1.1 C++ Standard Library

C++ Standard Library uses templated classes and objects to provide a wide range of capabilities. We will use the C++ standard library throughout the book. We will study classes and objects in detail in Part 2 of this book. For now, to use the library, we should remember that:

- Classes are user defined data types that consist of both data and methods (functions).

- The data type used by a templated class is specified in angle brackets <>. For example, aClass<int>.

- Objects are variables of a class which are created just like we create variables of built-in data types such as int.

- Objects call methods of their class to perform actions. The methods are called using the syntax anObject.aMethod(parameters).

C++ standard library is implemented in namespace std. Therefore, the std:: prefix is used to access the contents of the library as shown in the Hello World! program.

1.2 Preprocessor Directives and Header Files

A statement such as #include starting with # is called a *preprocessor directive*. Everything used in a C++ program must be declared before it is used. For example, we have used std::cout, std::endl, << and EXIT_SUCCESS in our program. The features provided with the C++ language are declared in *header files* (also called *include files*). To use any of these features, the header file in which that feature is declared must be included in our program using the #include directive. The #include directive tells the C++ compiler to merge the contents of the specified file with the current program file starting at the location of the #include. In our program, EXIT_SUCCESS is declared in the header file <cstdlib> while the other elements are declared in the header file <iostream>.

1.3 Statements and Comments

A *statement* is a description of an action we want to perform in our program. C++ statements end with a ";". In our program, we have a statement that prints a message on the screen using std::cout and a statement that returns the value EXIT_SUCCESS. You can write a statement using as many lines as you want as long as it ends with a ";".

Comments are used to describe what we are doing in the program. The comments are meant only for documentation. The C++ compiler ignores all comments. Comments begin with the // tag and everything on a line beginning with the // tag until the end of the line is treated as a comment. A comment can be on a separate line or in the same line as a statement.

1.4 Functions

A *function* is a named group of statements that start with an opening brace "{" and end with a closing brace "}". The group of statements between braces is the *body* of a function. In our program, we have a function named `main` which returns a value of type of `int` and which does not take any input parameters (the keyword `void` means none).

Every C++ program must contain one function named `main`. When we run a program, the system automatically calls the function `main`.

1.5   Programming Cycle

C++ is a compiled language. The steps involved in creating a C++ program are as follows:

1. **Edit**: We write our program using a text editor and store it in a file with extension `cpp`. For example, our Hello World! program will be stored in a file called `hello.cpp`. This is the *source file* of our program. A program may consist of several source files.

2. **Compile**: Compile the source files using a C++ compiler. The compiler will produce an *object module* (a file with extension `obj`) for each source file. For our program, the compiler will generate a file named `hello.obj`.

3. **Link**: Link the object modules using a linker to create an *executable file* with an extension `exe`. For our program, the linker will generate a file called `hello.exe`.

4. **Test**: Run the executable file by typing "`hello`" at the command prompt. It should print the message "`Hello World!`" on the screen.

If we want to make any change to our program, we have to repeat all four steps shown above: edit, compile, link and test.

2   Fundamentals

This chapter describes the basic building blocks of C++ programs.

2.1   Data Types

The standard data types used in C++ are:

Type	Comments
short int	We can use the designation short
int	The default integral type
long int	We can use the designation long
long long int	We can use the designation long long
unsigned short int	We can use the designation unsigned short
unsigned int	We can use the designation unsigned int
unsigned long int	We can use the designation unsigned long
float	IEEE Single precision number
double	IEEE Double precision number
long double	Extended precision number
char	Character
bool	true (1) or false (0)
auto	The compiler decides the type based on data type of the value

2.1.1   Storage size

The storage size of most data types is compiler or machine dependent. However, C++ also provides definitions of compiler independent fixed size standard types in header file <cstdint>. For example:

```
std::int8_t    // 8-bit integer
std::int16_t   // 16-bit integer
std::int32_t   // 32-bit integer
std::int64_t   // 64-bit integer
```

Please see your compiler documentation for more definitions.

2.1.2   Limits

The C++ header files `<climits>` and `<cfloat>` define the largest and smallest values for integral and float types. For example, constant `INT_MIN` is the minimum value for an `int` and `INT_MAX` the maximum. The best way to access the limits is using the header file `<limits>` and templated `numeric_limits` interface as shown below:

```
#include <cstdlib>
#include <iostreams>
#include <limits>

std::cout << "lowest int = "
          << std::numeric_limits<int>::lowest() << std::endl;
std::cout << "max int = "
          << std::numeric_limits<int>::max() << std::endl;

std::cout << "lowest double = "
          << std::numeric_limits<double>::lowest() << std::endl;
std::cout << "max double = "
          << std::numeric_limits<double>::max() << std::endl;
```

Other limits can be queried in the same way.

2.1.3   Conversions between Data Types

The C++ compiler automatically converts values of one data type into another using *standard conversions*.

Conversions from short to int, short to long, long to float, float to double, etc. that involve a widening of the size of the value are done automatically without informing the user because it can be done without loss of information. This is called *promoting* the value.

Conversions that involve a narrowing of the size of the value from a larger to shorter size may result in loss of information and, therefore, require an *explicit conversion* or are performed by the compiler with a warning that there may be a loss of information. Explicit conversions between data types are done using *type casting*. For example, to use a `double` quantity as a `long`, we will use the statement

```
double d = 20000.0;
long x   = (long)d;               // method 1
long y   = static_cast<long>(d);  // method2 for built-in types
```

The value of d is converted into long and assigned to x and y. The value stored in d itself is not changed. In the example shown above there will be no loss of information because the specified value of d is within the range of long. In general, however, such conversions must be done with care.

2.2   Literal Constants

A value such as the number 123.45 in a program is referred to as a *literal constant*. Literal constants have a data type associated with them. The value of a literal is stored somewhere in the computer memory but we do not know its location. The location of a value in computer memory is called its *address*. Literal constants are *non-addressable*.

2.2.1   Literal Numbers

By default, an integer literal constant is treated as an int and a floating point literal constant is treated as a double. The data type of a literal constant can be declared to be of a different type by appending a letter at its end as follows:

```
123      // int
123U     // unsigned int
123L     // long
123UL    // unsigned long
123S     // short
123US    // unsigned short
123.4    // double
123.4F   // float
123.4L   // long double
```

An integer literal constant can be written using decimal (the default), octal or hexadecimal notation:

```
20       // decimal
020      // octal. Any literal beginning with 0
0x20     // hexadecimal. Any literal beginning with 0x
```

2.2.2 Literal Characters

A printable literal character constant is enclosed in single quotes:

```
'a'    'e'    'i'    'o'    'u'    ' '(space)
```

Non-printable literal characters are represented by an *escape sequence* of the form \xxx, where xxx is an octal number of up to three digits representing the ASCII value of the character. For example, the escape sequence \0 is NULL. Some predefined escape sequences are as follows:

```
\n    newline
\t    horizontal tab
\v    vertical tab
\b    backspace
\r    carriage return
\f    form feed
\a    bell
\\    back slash
\'    single quote
\"    double quote
```

2.2.3 String Literals

A string literal constant is zero or more characters enclosed in double quotes:

```
"We hold these truths to be self-evident ..."
""    // a NULL string
"a"   // string containing only one character
```

A string consists of the characters the string plus a NULL character (\0) added at the end by the compiler. The size of a string is, therefore, one more than the number of characters in the string. For example, the string "a" above has two characters ('a' and \0) and is not the same as the character literal 'a'.

2.3 Variables

Variables are named entities used to store *addressable* values of a particular data type. There are two values associated with each variable:

1. A named *lvalue*: The lvalue is a named entity storing the address of the magnitude of the variable. The name of a variable refers to its lvalue.

2. An unnamed *rvalue*: An rvalue is the magnitude of the variable. It is accessed using the address stored in the lvalue of the variable.

Variables are the building blocks for statements and expressions used in C++ programs.

2.3.1   Variable Names

The C++ specification requires that the maximum length of the name of a variable be at least 1024 characters long. The first character must be a letter while the rest may be letters, numbers or the underscore character '_'. The names are case sensitive: lower and upper case letters are treated as different characters. You should use descriptive names for your variables. Some examples of C++ names are:

```
velocity            // OK
Velocity            // OK. Not the same as velocity.
8Ball               // invalid. Starts with a number.
priceOfTea          // OK
price_of_tea        // OK
aCar                // OK
```

Always name your variables using a naming convention to make your programs easier to read and understand. The most common convention used today is *word capitalization*: the first word in a variable name is in lower case and the first letter of the remaining words is capitalized. Variables `velocity`, `aCar` and `priceOfTea` shown above follow this convention.

2.3.2   Declaring Variables

The name and the type of a variable must be specified before we use it in our program. This is called a *variable declaration*. A variable may also be assigned an initial value when it is declared. Storage for a variable is assigned when it is declared. Multiple variables of the same data type can be declared in the same declaration. Examples of variables declaration statements are:

```
int x;                   // declare x
double velocity = 10.0;  // declare and initialize velocity to
                         // 10.0
int x = 10, y, z = x;    // initialize x and z but not y
```

```
float priceOfTea;              // declare priceOfTea
```

A declaration statement is read from right to left. The first statement is read as follows: a variable named x which is of type int. It is good practice to describe the purpose of a variable by using a comment as shown above.

Because a statement can be written using as many lines as we want, a statement declaring multiple variables can also be written as follows:

```
short numberOfStates,     // number of states in a country
      cars,               // number of cars
      apples;             // number of apples
```

This format allows us to include comments with a multiple declaration.

2.4   Pointers

Pointers are variables in which the address of an rvalue is stored: the pointer *points* to the rvalue. As mentioned before, the name of a variable refers to the address of its rvalue. Therefore, the name of a variable is a pointer that points to its rvalue. A pointer has a type: it is the type of data value to which it points. For example, a pointer of type **double** will hold the address of a **double** rvalue.

Pointer variables are declared by prefixing the *dereferencing operator*, *, to the name of the variable. Examples of pointer variables are:

```
double *pVelocity         // a double pointer
char   *label;            // a char pointer
int    *pInt1, *pInt2, int3   ;  // two int pointers and an int
```

When declaring multiple pointer variables in a comma separated list, every pointer variable must be prefixed by *. For example, in the declaration statements shown above, pInt1 and pInt2 are pointers to an int while int3 is an int.

A pointer is assigned the address of an rvalue of the same type as the pointer using the *address of* operator, &, as shown below:

```
double speed, velocity     // declare speed and velocity
double *pSpeed = &speed;   // pSpeed points to speed
        pSpeed = &velocity; // pSpeed now points to velocity
```

The rvalue of a variable is accessed indirectly through a pointer using the dereferencing operator *:

```
double speed, velocity;    // declare speed and velocity
double *pSpeed = &speed;   // declare pointer to speed
```

```
*speed    = 10.0;        // same as speed = 10.0
*pSpeed   = 20.0;        // same as speed = 20.0
velocity = *pSpeed;      // same as velocity = speed
```

Note that both *speed and *pSpeed are used to access the rvalue of speed because the name of variable also points to its rvalue.

2.4.1   Special Pointers

A null pointer is a pointer with a value of nullptr. It is a pointer that does not point to any rvalue.

A void* can be used to store the address of any type of data value.

2.4.2   Pointer Arithmetic

Pointer arithmetic is used to access sets of data stored in contiguous locations in memory. You can add or subtract integer values to a pointer. The integer quantity is called the *offset* into the pointer. For example:

```
int *pNumber;
pNumber++;               //  increment int pointer by 1

double *pSpeed;
pSpeed = pspeed - 4;  //  decrement double pointer by 4
```

The address value stored in pNumber will be increased by an amount equal to the size of int data type: pNumber will now point to the next integer in a set of integers stored in contiguous locations in memory. The value of pSpeed will be decreased by an amount equal to 4 times the size of double data type: pSpeed will now point to the double value located four positions back from the current position in a set of double values stored in contiguous locations in memory. In this way, pointer arithmetic can be used to move backwards and forward through data sets stored in contiguous locations in memory.

2.4.3   Pointers Summary

- Pointers store the address of the *rvalue* of a variable.
- We can have null pointers that do not point to anything.

- The dereferencing operator * is used to access the rvalue that a pointer points to.

- The value stored in a pointer can be changed to point to a different rvalue.

2.5 References

A *reference* is an *alias* for a variable. A reference is not a copy of the variable it refers to, but a different name for the same variable. A reference is declared using the *address of* operator & and must be associated with a variable when it is declared. This association cannot be changed.

A reference must be initialized when it is declared except when:

- It is declared as an **extern** reference, i.e. it is initialized at another location.

- It is a member of a class.

- It is declared as a parameter in a function call.

- It is declared as a return type of a function.

The example below shows the use of references:

```cpp
#include <iostream>
#include <cstdlib>

// the main function
int main()
{
    long aVariable = 123;           // aVariable
    long& refVariable = aVariable;  // reference to aVariable

    // both statements output 123
    std::cout << aVariable << std::endl;
    std::cout << refVariable << std::endl;

    // a change in aVariable also reflected by refVariable
    aVariable = 1000 * aVariable;
    std::cout << aVariable    << std::endl;  // prints 123000
    std::cout << refVariable << std::endl;   // prints 123000

    refMyVariable = 1000;  // no de-referencing syntax
    std::cout << aVariable    << std::endl;  // prints 1000
```

```
    std::cout << refVariable << std::endl;   // prints 1000

    return EXIT_SUCCESS;
}
```

As we can see, all operations on either refVariable or aVariable act on aVariable.

In summary, a reference

- Acts like another name for an existing variable. Therefore, we cannot have a NULL reference.

- A reference must be initialized when it is created.

- A reference cannot be reassigned to another variable.

- A reference does not use a de-referencing operator to access the rvalue of the variable.

- A reference does not allocate new memory for storage because it refers to an existing variable.

2.6 Named Constants

Most programs need to use addressable values that are constant i.e. which cannot be changed after they are set. These named constants, called *symbolic constants*, are defined by declaring constant variables using the keyword const or by using the preprocessor directive #define. Constant declarations are usually placed in a header file.

2.6.1 Using #define

Named constants may be defined using the preprocessor directive #define:

```
#define PI        3.1418
#define aString   "A Constant String"
```

The C++ compiler provides several constants using #define such as EXIT_SUCCESS that we have already used.

2.6.2   const Variables

Constants variables are defined using the keyword const as follows:

```
double const PI = 3.1418;
char const * const aString = "A Constant String";
char const * aString       = "A Constant String";
char * const aString       = "A Constant String Pointer";
```

The statements above are read from right to left as follows:

- **First statement**: A variable named PI which is a constant of type double. Once declared, the value of variable PI cannot be changed.

- **Second statement**: A variable named aString which is a constant pointer to a constant of type char. Once declared, we cannot change the address stored in aString or the character stored at that address. Both are declared constant.

- **Third statement**: A variable named aString which is a pointer to a constant of type char. Once declared, we can change the address in aString to point to another character but we cannot change the character stored at the address using aString.

- **Fourth statement**: A variable named aString which is a constant pointer to a char. Once declared, we cannot change the address stored in aString but we can change the character stored at that address. Only the address is declared const.

We may also declare constant references to variables:

```
long aVariable;                          // not a const
long const &refVariable = aVariable;  // reference to const long
```

In this case, the contents of aVariable cannot be changed using refVariable but you can change aVariable itself:

```
aVariable = aVariable + 1;       // OK
refVariable = refVariable + 1;  // error
```

Using constant variables is preferable to the use of preprocessor directive #define.

2.6.3 Enumerations

An *Enumeration* is an ordered set of mnemonic names assigned to a set of values of any integral type. Enumerations are declared using the keyword enum:

```
enum class enumName : type { enumerators };
```

The data type is optional and is assumed to be int if it is not specified. Examples of enumerations are given below:

```
enum class Color {red, green, blue};
enum class Materials {Iron=1, Steel, Copper=10, Brass};
```

Color and Materials now become data types with a fixed set of values that cannot be changed. Unless specified otherwise, the values declared in the list are initialized with an integer code starting with 0. In the enum Color above, the value of red is 0, green is 1 and blue is 2. Specific values can also be specified in the declaration. In Materials, value of Iron is 1, Steel is 2, Copper is 10 and Brass is 11.

The values of an enumeration are scoped and must be qualified by the name of the enumeration. The enumeration values are not automatically converted into a value of its type nor can a value of its type be assigned to an enumeration. Explicit casts are required for conversions. For example:

```
Materials aMaterial = Steel;              // error
Materials aMaterial = Materials::Steel;   // OK

int gadget = aMaterial;                   // error
int gadget = static_cast<int>(aMaterial;) // OK. gadget = 2

Materials aMaterial = 2;                           // Error
Materials aMaterial = static_cast<Materials::Steel>(2); // OK
```

2.7 Operators

All operations in C++ are performed using *operators*. The objects on which operations are performed are called *operands*. Operators that act on one operand are called *unary operators* while those that act on two operands (called the *left* and *right* operands) are called *binary operators*. C++ has a number of operators built into the language for the standard data types. When the left and right operands of a binary operator are of different types, the C++ compiler automatically converts the type of one of the operands using standard conversions.

2.7.1 Assignment Operator

The *assignment operator* = alters the values of a variable or an object without changing its type. The value of the right operand is copied into the left operand. Therefore, the left operand must be an *lvalue*. For example,

```
int x, y;      // declare x and y as int
double a, b;   // declare a and b as double

x = 1;         // assign the value of 1 to x
y = 1.5;       // y is 1. Narrowed by truncation to int
a = 2.0        // assign the value 2.0 to a
b = 5;         // b = 5.0. Widened by conversion to double
```

When assigning a value to a floating point number as shown above for variable a, always use **2.0** not 2 as you would for an integer.

2.7.2 Arithmetic Operators

Arithmetic operators in C++ are:

- Add (+)
- Subtract (-)
- Multiply (*)
- Divide (/)
- Modulus (%)

These operators work as shown below:

```
int x = 20, y = 7, z;  // declare x, y and z as int
double a, b;

z = x * y;        // value of z will be 140
z = x % y;        // value of z will be 6. Remainder of x/y.
z = x + y;        // value of z will be 27
z = x - y;        // value of z will be 13
z = x / y;        // value of z will be 2 not 2.86
a = x;            // value of a set to 20.0
```

```
b = a / y;              // value of b will be 2.86
```

When the two operands are not of the same data type, the compiler performs standard type conversions using promotion to ensure that both operands in an arithmetic operation are of the same type. When we divide x by y, no conversions take place because both operands are of type int. The compiler performs integer division of 20 by 7 and assigns it to z. When the value of x is assigned to a, the compiler automatically promotes x to double without changing its stored value and assigns the result to a. When, we divide a by y, the compiler promotes y to double before performing the division. The result, a double quantity, is assigned to b.

2.7.3   Updating Assignment Operators

C++ also provides *updating assignment operators* that combine assignment and arithmetic operators:

- += : Addition
- -= : Subtraction
- *= : Multiplication
- /= : Division
- %= : Modulo

For example, the statements:

```
int x = 10;
x = x + 10;   // x is now 20
```

can be written as:

```
int x = 10;
x += 10;      // x is now 20
```

The operator adds the value of the right operand to the value of the left operand and stores the result in the left operand. The other updating operators work in the same way.

2.7.4   Increment and Decrement Operators

C++ also provides *increment* (++) and *decrement* (--) operators to increase or decrease the value of a variable by 1. Each has a *prefix* and *postfix* form, resulting in four operators: pre-increment, post-increment, pre-decrement and post-decrement. These operators work as follows:

```
int x = 10, y;

y = ++x; // Pre-increment: x increased by one before
         // it is assigned to y.
         // Therefore, now y = 11 and x = 11
y = x++; // Post-increment: x increased by one after it
         // is assigned to y.
         // Therefore, now y = 10 and x = 11
y = --x; // Pre-decrement: x decreased by one before it
         // is assigned to y.
         // Therefore, y = 9 and x = 9
y = x--; // Post-decrement: x decreased by one after it
         // is assigned to y.
         // Therefore, y = 10 and x = 9
```

The statement y = ++x is equivalent to:

```
x = x + 1;
y = x;
```

The statement y = x++ is equivalent to:

```
y = x;
x = x + 1;
```

The decrement operators work the same way.

2.7.5   Relational Operators

Relational operators are used to perform comparisons. The comparisons return a value of type bool:

- Less than (<): Returns true only if the left operand is less than the right operand.

- Less than or equal to (<=): Returns true only if the left operand is less than or equal to the right operand.

- Greater than (>): Returns true only if the left operand is greater than the right operand.

- Greater than or equal to (>=): Returns true only if the left operand is greater than or equal to the right operand.

- Equals (==): Returns **true** only if the left operand is equal to the right operand.

- Not equals (!=): Returns **true** only if the left operand is not equal to the right operand.

The operands are evaluated from left to right. In C++, any value that does not evaluate to **false** is true. Therefore, any nonzero integral value is evaluates to true. However, the keyword **true** is defined as **1**.

2.7.6   Logical Operators

Logical operators available in C++ are:

- Negation (!): A unary operator. The ! operator evaluates to **true** if its operand is **false**. Otherwise it is **false**.

- AND (&&): The && operator returns **true** only if both its operands are **true**. Otherwise it is **false**.

- OR (||): The || operator returns **false** only if both of its operands are **false**. Otherwise, it is **true**.

The operands are evaluated from left to right.

2.7.7   sizeof Operator

The **sizeof** operator return the size (in bytes) of an object or the result of an expression. For example:

```
sizeof(int)      // returns size of int
sizeof(double)   // returns size of double
```

The operator is used frequently for memory management.

2.7.8   Operator Precedence and Associativity

When several operators are used together in a compound expression, the order in which operations are performed is determined by the precedence and associativity of the operators:

- Operators are evaluated in the order of highest to lowest precedence.

- The evaluation order for operators with equal precedence is determined by their associativity: left to right or right to left.

Precedence can be overridden by the use of parenthesis to create sub-expressions within the main expression. When evaluating compound expression, the first step is to evaluate all sub-expressions.

Precedence and associativity of some of the common operators is given below in order of decreasing precedence:

C++ Operator	Purpose	Associativity
. ->	Member selection	Left to right
[]	Subscripting	Left to right
()	Function Call Operator	Left to Right
++	Post-increment	Left to Right
--	Post-decrement	Left to Right
sizeof	Object size	Right to Left
++	Pre-increment	Right to Left
--	Pre-decrement	Right to left
* & + - !	Unary operators	Right to left
new	Create object	Right to left
delete	Delete object	Right to left
(type)	Type Casting	Right to Left
* / %	Multiplicative Operators	Left to Right
+ -	Additive Operators	Left to Right
< > <= >=	Relational Operators	Left to Right
== !=	Equality Operators	Left to Right
&&	Logical AND	Left to Right
||	Logical OR	Left to Right
= *= /= += -= %=	Assignment Operators	Right to Left

2.8 Expressions

An *expression* is composed of variables, constants and one or more operators. When two or more operators are combined the expression is called a *compound expression*. Some examples of expressions are:

```
int w, x = 20, y = 5, z = 25;

w = x*y - z;        // value of w is 75
x < z;              // true. The value of expression is 1
y == x;             // false. The value of expression is 0
x > y && y < z;     // true because both clauses are true.
                    // Value of this expression is 1
x > z && y < z;     // false because first clause is false.
                    // Value of this expression is 0
x > z || y < z;     // true because second clause is true.
                    // Value of this expression is 1
x < y || y > z;     // false because both clauses are false.
                    // Value of this expression is 0
```

2.9 Statements

A *statement* is the smallest unit of execution in a program. All statements end with a semicolon. Different types of statements are as follows:

- A declaration followed by a semicolon is a *declaration statement* and is the only statement that can be specified outside a function.

- An expression followed by a semicolon is an *expression statement*.
  ```
  int marks;    // a declaration statement
  marks += 10;  // an expression statement
  ;             // a null statement
  ```

- A *compound statement* is a sequence of statements enclosed in braces:
  ```
  {
  int marks;    // a declaration statement
  marks += 10;  // an expression statement
  std::cout << marks << endl;
  }
  ```
  The compound statement is treated as a unit and may be placed anywhere in a program. A compound statement that contains one or

more declaration statements is called a *statement block*. The statement blocks can be nested.

The normal flow of a program is sequential starting from the first statement in the program and proceeding to the end.

2.10 Scope and Lifetime of Variables

The *scope* of a variable is the section of code in which it can be accessed. The *lifetime* of a variable is the time during which it exists – i.e. its address is valid.

A *static* variable is stored in the data segment of an object file and is *global* in scope within the source file in which it is declared. The variable is available for the duration of the program.

A non-static *local variable* declared in a statement block is visible to all code following the point in the code where it is declared, including all statement blocks nested within the block after the point of declaration. A local variable is not visible outside the block in which it is declared. If a nested statement block declares a local variable having the same name and type as a variable in the enclosing statement block, the newly declared variable *hides* the variable in the enclosing block.

```
int x, y;      // declare x and y as int

x = 10;        // x is 10
y = 50;        // y is 50

{              // a nested statement block
    int x;     // this declaration hides x defined in
               // enclosing statement block
    x = 20;    // this block x = 20. Outer block x = 10
}

x = 30;        // outer block x now 30. Inner block x
               // destroyed
```

Local variables are created and stored in the *function call stack* when program execution enters the statement block in which they are declared and are destroyed when execution leaves the block. That is why they are also called *automatic variables*.

2.11 Making Decisions

The linear flow of a program can be changed using *control of flow* statements. The statements that enable us to do so are `if` and `switch` statements.

2.11.1 The if Statement

The structure of an `if` statement is as follows:

```
if(expression)
  {
    // Execute this block if expression is true
    if statement block;
  }

statement;   // jump here if expression is false
```

If the expression evaluates to `true`, the statement block following the `if` statement is executed. Otherwise, the block is ignored and the first statement after the `if` statement block is executed.

An either-or condition is expressed by combining an `else` clause with the `if` statement:

```
if(expression)
  {
    // Execute this block if expression is true
    if statement block;
  }
else
  {
    // Execute this block if expression is false
    else statement block;
  }
```

If the `expression` evaluates to `true`, the `if` statement block is executed. Otherwise, the `else` statement block is executed.

A third form of the `if` statements can be used to test for multiple conditions:

```
if(expression1)
  {
    if statement block;
  }
else if(expression2)
```

```
  {
    else-if statement block;
  }


  ...


else      // this else block is optional
  {
    else statement block;
  }
```

In this case, the statement block corresponding to the **expression** that evaluates to **true** is executed. If none of the expressions is **true**, no action is taken or the statement block for the optional **else** block is executed if one is provided.

2.11.2 If Statement Example

The use of an **if-else-if** statement is illustrated below:

```cpp
#include <cstdlib>
#include <iostream>

// the main function
int main()
{
    int choice;

    std::cout << "Choose your language: " << std::endl;
    std::cout << "   C++ :  Enter 1" << std::endl;
    std::cout << "   C   :  Enter 2" << std::endl;
    std::cout << "   Java:  Enter 3" << std::endl;
    std::cout << "   Basic: Enter 4" << std::endl;
    std::cout << "Enter your choice: ";
    std::cin >> choice;

    if(choice == 1)
      {
        std::cout << "I love C++" << std::endl;
      }
    else if(choice == 2)
      {
        std::cout << "I love C" << std::endl;
      }
```

```
  else if(choice == 3)
    {
      std::cout << "I love Java" << std::endl;
    }
  else if(choice == 4)
    {
      std::cout << "I love Basic" << std::endl;
    }
  else
    {
      std::cout << "None of the above" << std::endl;
    }

  return EXIT_SUCCESS;
}
```

2.11.3 The switch Statement

The switch statement provides a method of choosing between mutually exclusive choices. The structure of the switch statement is as follows:

```
switch(expression)
{
 case constantValue1:
   compound statement 1;
   break;

 case constantValue2:
   compound statement 2;
   break;

 ...

 case constantValueN:
   compound statement N;
   break;

 default:       // in case no match is found (optional)
   default statements;
}
```

The expression must evaluate to an integral or a character data type. The value of expression is compared with the constant values specified in the case labels until a match is found or all labels have been checked. If a match is found, execution begins with the first statement after the label and continues until a `break` statement is encountered or the end of `switch` statement is reached. If no match is found, either no action is taken or, if an optional `default` label is provided, statements after the `default` label are executed.

2.11.4 Switch Statement Example

An example of a `switch` statement using an enumeration is given below:

```
#include <cstdlib>
#include <iostream>

enum class Language : char { CPP, C, Java, Basic };

// the main function
int main()
{
    Language myFavorite;
    int choice;

    std::cout << "Choose your language: " << std::endl;
    std::cout << "    C++:   Enter 1" << std::endl;
    std::cout << "    C#:    Enter 2" << std::endl;
    std::cout << "    Java:  Enter 3" << std::endl;
    std::cout << "    Basic: Enter 4" << std::endl;
    std::cout << "Enter your choice: ";
    std::cin >> choice;
    myFavorite = (Language)--choice; // decrement choice by 1

    switch( myFavorite )
      {
      case Language::CPP:
         std::cout << "I love C++" << std::endl;
         break;
      case Language::Java:
         std::cout << "I love Java" << std::endl;
      case Language::C:
         std::cout << "I love C" << std::endl;
         break;
      case Language::Basic:
         std::cout << "I love Basic" << std::endl;
```

```
        break;
    default:
        std::cout << "None of the above" << std::endl;
        break;
    }

    return EXIT_SUCCESS;
}
```

The integer input by the user is converted into the enumeration Language. The switch statement works as follows:

- If input is 1, the case C++ block is used and the program prints "I love C++" and the break statement transfers control to the end of the switch statement.

- If input is 2, the program prints both "I love Java" and "I love C#" because there is no break statement after case Java and the execution continues until the break statement of case C# is encountered.

- If input is 3, only "I love C#" is printed.

- If input is 4, only "I love Basic" is printed.

- For all other input, the default case is invoked and "None of the above" is printed.

2.12 Performing Repetitive Tasks

Repetitive tasks are performed using *iterative statements* for, do-while and while loops. All loops use a loop termination condition to end the loop and, therefore, we have to ensure that the loop termination condition is satisfied at some point during loop execution.

2.12.1 The for Loop

A for loop combines loop initialization, loop termination condition and loop incrementing into one statement as follows:

```
for(initialization;
    loop termination condition;
    loop increment statements)
    {
```

```
    statement block;   // body of loop
    }
```

A simple **for** loop is shown below:

```
for(int i = 0; i < 10; ++i)
    {
    statement block;     // body of loop
    }
```

The loop works as follows:

1. **Initialization statement**: This statement is executed only once, when the **for** statement is started. The loop variable **i** is declared in the initialization statement itself and initialized to 0. The scope of **i** is the body of the loop. Any number of variables can be initialized in this statement by using a comma separated list. Variables initialized in this statement do not have to be declared in the initialization statement itself.

2. **Loop termination condition**: This condition is checked at the top of the loop. If it evaluates to **true**, the body of the loop is executed. If it is **false**, the loop ends. If the condition is **false** when the loop is started, the body of the loop will never be executed.

3. **The increment statement**: This statement is executed at the bottom of the loop and the control returns to the top of the loop where step 2 is performed. Any number of variables can be incremented by using a comma separated list.

The example below shows how a **for** loop may be used to calculate an average value of a set of numbers:

```
#include <cstdlib>
#include <iostream>

// the main function
int main()
{
    long howMany;          // how many numbers to input

    double sum = 0.0,
           number = 0.0,
           average = 0.0;

    std::cout << "How many numbers? ";
    std::cin  >> howMany;
```

```
for(int i = 0; i < howMany; ++i)
   {
      std::cout << "Input number #" << i+1 << ": ";
      std::cin  >> number;

      sum += number;
   }

average = sum / howMany;
std::cout << std::endl << "Average is " << average
         << std::endl;

return EXIT_SUCCESS;
}
```

Another variation of the **for** loop can be used with arrays or other collections of data:

```
int[] array = { 1, 2, 3, 4, 5 };
for(int& aValue : array)
{
   statement block;   // do something with aValue
}
```

The **for** statement is read as follows: for each **int** element **aValue** contained in **array**, execute the statements in the statement block.

2.12.2 The do-while Loop

The structure of a **do-while** loop is as follows:

```
do
   {
     statement block;    // body of loop
   } while(expression);
```

The **expression** is checked at the bottom of the loop. Therefore, the statements in the body of the loop are always executed at least once. The loop is executed repeatedly as long as the **expression** at the bottom of the loop evaluates to **true**.

2.12.3 The while Loop

The structure of a while loop is as follows:

```
while(expression)
   {
     statement block;    // body of loop
   }
```

The statements in the body of the loop are executed repeatedly as long as the expression at the top of the loop evaluates to true. If the expression is false the first time, statements in body of the loop are never executed.

2.12.4 The break and continue Statements

The break and continue statements change the normal operation of for, do-while and while loops. The break statement terminates the loop and transfers control to the first statement after the end of the loop. The continue statement skips the execution of the remaining statements for the current iteration and transfers control back to the top of the loop.

We will change our average calculating program to use break and continue statements such that:

1. Numbers between 10 and 20 are not used in the average calculation

2. Input is terminated if the user inputs a number greater than 30,000

The modified program is given below:

```
#include <cstdlib>
#include <iostream>

// the main function
int main()
{
   short howMany,           // how many numbers to input
         numbersUsed = 0; // numbers used in calculations

   double sum = 0.0,
          number = 0.0,
          average = 0.0;

   std::cout << "How many numbers? ";
   std::cin  >> howMany;
```

```
std::cout << std::endl
          << "To stop input at any time" << std::endl
          << "enter a number > 30,000\n" << std::endl;

for(int i = 0; i < howMany; ++i)
   {
     std::cout << "Input number #" << i+1 << ": ";
     std::cin  >> number;

     if(number > 30000)
        {
          break;         // end loop and calculate average
        }
     if(number >= 10 && number <= 20)
        {
          continue;      // go to top of loop
        }

     sum += number;      // calculate sum
     numbersUsed++;      // count of numbers added
   }

average = sum / numbersUsed;
std::cout << std::endl << "Average of " << numbersUsed
          << " numbers is " << average
          << std::endl;

return EXIT_SUCCESS;
}
```

The changes are highlighted in bold.

Sometimes, having the loop termination condition checked at the top or bottom of the loop is not convenient. We can use the break statement to position the loop termination condition anywhere in our logic:

```
int iterations = 0;    // keep count of iterations
while(true)             // always true
   {
     statement block;

     if(iterations > 100)
        {
          break;              // end loop if iterations > 100
        }
```

```
    statement block;

    iterations++;        // increment counter

    statement block;
  }
```

By specifying **true** or a nonzero constant in the **while** expression, we set up a loop that runs forever. Such loops are called *infinite loops*. Such loops can only be terminated by a **break** statement located somewhere in the body of the loop. It is up to us to ensure that our program logic will invoke the **break** statement at some time during the execution of the loop or the loop will never end. In the code shown above, we have to ensure that the value of **iterations** is greater than **100** at some point during the execution of the loop.

An infinite **for** loop can be set up by using null statements in its definition as shown below:

```
for( ; ; )
  {
  // an infinite for loop
  statement block;
  }
```

2.13 Arrays

An array is an ordered collection of objects of the same type. Individual elements, called *array elements*, are not named individually but are accessed by using a numeric *index* or *subscript* that specifies the position of the element in the collection. The number of indices used to specify an array element is called its *dimension*.

2.13.1 Single Dimension Array

A single dimension array is declared as follows:

```
int numbers[10];  // int array named numbers with 10 elements
```

The number of elements in an array is specified within brackets following the name of the array. The elements of an array are numbered starting from 0: for an array with 10 elements, the index values are 0 through 9. In the above example, `numbers[0]` is the first element, `numbers[5]` the sixth and `numbers[9]` the tenth. The elements of an array may be used in expressions as follows:

```
int aNumber;
numbers[5] = 10;        // sixth array element = 10
aNumber = numbers[5];   // aNumber = sixth array element
```

An array may be initialized when it is declared using a comma separated list of values enclosed in braces:

```
int numbers[]  = {10, 25, 60, 70};
int numbers[5] = {10, 25, 60, 70};
```

The first statement creates and initializes an array of four elements. The second statement creates an array with five elements and initializes the first four elements with the values given in the list. The fifth element is automatically initialized to 0.

2.13.2 Multidimensional Arrays

Multidimensional arrays are defined with each dimension specified with its own brackets. For example, the statement

```
int numbers[4][3];
```

declares a two-dimensional array `numbers` with dimensions 4 and 3. The first dimension is called the *row dimension* and the second the *column dimension*: the numbers array has 4 rows and 3 columns. Multidimensional arrays can also be initialized at declaration:

```
int numbers[4][3] = { {0, 1, 2},
                      {3, 4, 5},
                      {6, 7, 8},
                      {9, 10, 11} };
int numbers[4][3] = { 0, 1, 2, 3, 4, 5,
                      6, 7, 8, 9, 10, 11 };
```

The two statements accomplish the same thing. However, the first syntax makes it clear that we are dealing with four rows, each having three elements. Individual elements of the array are accessed using a bracket for each dimension:

```
int aNumber;
int numbers[4][3] = { {0, 1, 2},
                      {3, 4, 5},
                      {6, 7, 8},
```

```
                          {9, 10, 11} };
aNumber = numbers[0][2];   // aNumber equal to 2
aNumber = numbers[3][0];   // aNumber equal to 9
aNumber = numbers[2][1];   // aNumber equal to 7
numbers[2][1] = 30;        // change the value from 7 to 30
```

When used in loops, the index of the rightmost bracket varies the fastest:

```
long sum;
int numbers[4][3] = { {0, 1, 2},
                      {3, 4, 5},
                      {6, 7, 8},
                      {9, 10, 11} };

for(int i = 0; i < 4; ++i)
   {
     sum = 0;
     for(int j = 0; i < 3; ++j)
        {
          sum += numbers[i][j];
        }
   }
```

We will change our average calculating program to use an array to store numbers input by the user:

```
#include <cstdlib>
#include <iostream>

// the main function
int main()
{
    short howMany,          // how many numbers to input
          numbersUsed = 0;  // numbers used in calculations

    double sum = 0.0,       // sum initialized to 0.0
           average = 0.0,   // average initialized to 0.0
           numbers[100];    // an array of dimension 100

    // input numbers into array
    std::cout << "How many numbers? ";
    std::cin  >> howMany;

    std::cout << std::endl
              << "To stop input at any time" << std::endl
              << "enter a number > 30,000\n" << std::endl;
```

```
    for(int i = 0; i < howMany; ++i)
      {
        std::cout << "Input number #" << i+1 << ": ";
        std::cin >> numbers[i];
        if(numbers[i] > 30000)
          {
            howMany = i;   // count of numbers in array
            break;         // end input loop
          }
      }

  // use array to calculate average
    for(int i = 0; i < howMany; ++i)
      {
        if(numbers[i] >= 10 && numbers[i] <= 20)
          {
            continue;        // go to top of loop
          }

        sum += numbers[i];   // calculate sum
        numbersUsed++;       // increment count of numbers
      }

    average = sum / numbersUsed;
    std::cout << std::endl << "Average of " << numbersUsed
              << " numbers is " << average
              << std::endl;

    return EXIT_SUCCESS;
}
```

The changes are highlighted in bold. All the marks input by the user are stored in an array and are available for use at any time in the program.

2.13.3 Pointers and Arrays

Pointers and arrays are closely related. When we declare an array as follows:

```
int numbers[5];
```

the name of the array, numbers, points to the first element in the array: the value dereferenced by *numbers is the same as the value of array element numbers[0]. Incrementing numbers by 1 will change the address value in numbers to point to the second element in the array: i.e. *(numbers++) is the same as numbers[1]. In general, *(numbers + i) is the same as numbers[i], where i is an integer. Conversely, the address value returned by &numbers[i] is the same as (numbers + i).

Pointer arithmetic is often used to step through an array. For example, the following code reverses the elements of an array:

```cpp
#include <cstdlib>
#include <iostream>

// the main function
int main()
{
  int x[10] = {1, 2, 3, 4, 5, 6, 7, 8, 9, 10}, // declare array
      temp;                // temp variable

  int *start = &x[0],   // point to first element
      *end = &x[9];     // point to last element

  // Loop while start points to a location in the array
  // that is before the location of the end pointer
  while(start < end)       // compare pointers
  {
      // store value pointed to by start in temp
      temp = *start;

      // Store value pointed to by end in start
      // Then use post-increment to point start to the
      // next element
      *start++ = *end;

      // store value in temp in end element.
      // Then use post-decrement to point end to the
      // previous element
      *end-- = temp;
  }
  return EXIT_SUCCESS;
}
```

Note the use of post-increment and post-decrement operators to step through the array.

It is up to us to ensure that the index value used in the array syntax or the pointer to an array element does go past the bounds of the array. The compiler does not check!

2.14 Strings

A *string* is a `char` array consisting of the characters in the string plus a terminating `NULL` character added at the end. Therefore, the size of the array used to store a string is one more than the number of characters in the string. All string manipulation is done using a `char*` pointing to the first character in the string array. The data type of a string literal is `char*`. Therefore we can assign a string literal to a `char*` as shown below:

```
char* car = "This is my car";
```

The pointer `car` points to the first character in the string: the data value stored at `*car` is `'T'`. Because a string is an array, pointer arithmetic can be used to access any character in the string: the expression `*car++` will access the second character `'h'`, `*(car+9)` the tenth character `'y'`, and so on. The characters in the string can also be accessed using array syntax: `car[0]` is `'T'`, `car[1]` is `'h'`, `car[9]` is `'y'`, and so on.

A character array can be changed into a string by providing the terminating `NULL` character. For example:

```
char anArray[5] = {'c', 'a', 'r', 's'}; // not a string

// set the fifth element to \0.
anArray[4] = '\0';  // array may be used as string "cars"

// set the third element to \0.
anArray[2] = '\0';  // array may be used as string "ca"
```

C++ provides several built-in functions that operate on strings. They all use `NULL` terminated strings as arguments. We will look at them in the chapter on functions.

2.15 C++ Containers

C++ Standard Template Library (STL) is a part of the C++ Standard Library. STL provides container classes to store similar objects of built-in or user-defined types. Types of containers include `array`, `vector`, `set`, `list`, `map` (dictionary), `multimap`, `queue` and `stack`. We will look at `vector`, `string` and `map` in more detail. Please consult the STL reference for your compiler for details on these and other containers.

2.15.1 Vector

Requires header file `<vector>`.

A `vector` is a dynamic container that automatically grows as required to store elements in the vector. The amount of memory currently allocated for a vector is called its *capacity*. Additional memory is allocated automatically when the capacity is exhausted. This allocation process has a negative impact on the performance of the vector. To avoid frequent reallocations, we can specify the amount of memory to be *reserved* for the vector. A `vector` is similar to built-in C++ arrays but is more flexible and powerful.

A vector to store integers is created as follows:

```
std::vector <int> aVector1;        // an empty int vector
std::vector <int> aVector2(50);    // an int vector with
                                   // size 50. Elements
                                   // not initialized.
std::vector <int> aVector3(50, 5); // an int vector with
                                   // size 50.
                                   // All elements set to 5.
```

Some capabilities of a `vector` are shown below:

```
// fill vector with values using [] operator. Bounds
// checking is not performed
for(int i = 0; i < aVector2.size(); ++i)
   {
     aVector2[i] = i;
   }

// add new element at the end of vector
aVector2.push_back(999);
```

```
// remove element at the end of vector
aVector2.pop_back();

// replace current elements with 10 elements with value 999
aVector2.assign(10, 999);

// element access
aVector2.at(3);    // returns reference to fourth element.
                   // bounds checking is performed.
aVector2.front();  // returns the first element
aVector2.back();   // returns the last element
aVector2.data();   // returns a raw pointer to data array

// capacity related operations
aVector.max_size();     // maximum possible number of elements
                        // that can be stored in the vector
aVector2.capacity();    // number of elements that can be
                        // stored in allocated memory
aVector2.reserve(900);  // increase capacity to 900 elements
aVector2.shrink_to_fit(); // set capacity equal to size.
                        // frees unused memory.

aVector2.size();        // number of elements in the vector
aVector2.resize(100);   // set size to 100
aVector2.clear();       // empty the vector. size set to 0
aVector2.empty()        // returns true if vector is empty
```

Vectors should be used instead of arrays for handling collections of large objects. Our average calculating program modified to use a **vector** is shown below:

```
#include <cstdlib>
#include <iostream>
#include <vector>

// the main function
int main()
{
    short howMany,          // how many numbers to input
          numbersUsed = 0,  // numbers used in calculations
          temp = 0;         // numbers used in calculations

    double sum = 0.0,       // sum initialized to 0.0
           average = 0.0;   // average initialized to 0.0

    std::vector<int> numbers;    // an empty vector
```

```
    // input numbers into vector
    std::cout << "How many numbers? ";
    std::cin  >> howMany;

    std::cout << std::endl
            << "To stop input at any time" << std::endl
            << "enter a number > 30,000\n" << std::endl;

    for(int i = 0; i < howMany; ++i)
       {
       std::cout << "Input number #" << i+1 << ": ";
       std::cin  >> temp;
       if(numbers[i] > 30000)
          {
          break;         // end input loop
          }
       numbers.push_back(temp);
       }

  // use vector to calculate average
    for(int i = 0; i < numbers.size(); ++i)
       {
       if(numbers[i] >= 10 && numbers[i] <= 20)
          {
          continue;       // go to top of loop
          }

       sum += numbers[i];  // calculate sum
       numbersUsed++;      // increment count of numbers
       }

    average = sum / numbersUsed;
    std::cout << std::endl << "Average of " << numbersUsed
            << " numbers is " << average
            << std::endl;

    return EXIT_SUCCESS;
}
```

The changes are highlighted in bold.

2.15.2 The string class

Requires header file <string>.

C++ Standard Library provides a string class as an alternative to using NULL terminated arrays as strings. A string object may be used just like a built-in C++ string. The real power comes from the functions provided by the string class as shown in the code fragment below:

```
std::string hello = "Hello";
std::string world("World");

hello += " ";  // hello is now "Hello ";
std::string greet = hello + world; // greet = "Hello World"

greet.compare("Hello World"); // result: (0 = same string)

greet.c_str();  // returns a const pointer to a C style
                // null terminated string.
                // Same as greet.data()
char buffer[10];
greet.copy(buffer, 8, 2);  // copy 8 characters from the
                           // string starting from index 2
                           // into buffer.
                           // buffer contains: "llo Worl"
std::string str = greet.substr(2, 8);  // extract 8 chars
                           // starting from index 2 to str.
                           // str contains: "llo Worl"

// character access: Supports indexed access with no
// bounds checking and provides a range checked at() function.
greet[2];         // 'l'
greet[2] = 'p';   // results in "Heplo World"

greet.at(3);      // 'l'. bounds checked.
greet.at(3) = 'x'; // results in "Hepxo World"
greet.front;      // returns first character
greet.back();     // returns last character

// string modification
greet.clear();           // erase all characters
greet.empty();           // true if string has no characters

greet.insert(0, "Msg: "); // insert "Msg: " at index 0
                          // result: "Msg: Hepxo World"
```

```
greet.insert(0, "1234 ", 2); // insert 2 characters
                             // from "1234" at index 0
                             // result: "12Msg: Hepxo World"
greet.erase(0, 2);           // remove 2 characters starting
                             // from index 0.
                             // result: "Msg: Hepxo World"
greet.append("!!");          // append characters. Same as +=
                             // result: "Msg: Hepxo World!!"
greet.replace(3, 2, "??");   // replace 2 characters
                             // starting at index 3 with "??"
                             // result: "Msg??Hepxo World!!"

greet.max_size();       // maximum possible size for a string
greet.capacity();       // number of characters that can be
                        // stored in allocated memory
greet.shrink_to_fit();  // free unused memory
greet.reserve(500);     // increases capacity to 500
greet.size();           // length of string. Same as length().
greet.resize(100);      // changes length of string to 100
                        // fills empty places with NULL

// Search
greet.find("Hep");      // find "Hep" in string. Result: 5
greet.find('o');        // find char 'o' in string. Result: 9
greet.find('o', 10);    // find char 'o' in string starting
                        // from index 10. Result: 12
greet.find('?');        // find char '?' in string.
                        // Result: 3
greet.rfind('?');       // find char '?' in string starting
                        // from end of string. Result: 4
```

The **string** class should be used instead of null terminated character arrays to avoid the problems inherent with using pointers and pointer arithmetic to manipulate data.

2.15.3 Map

Requires header file `<map>`.

A **map** associates a unique *key* with a *value*. The *key*/*value* pairs are indexed and sorted automatically based on the key. The value of a key cannot be changed but the value associated with it can be. To change a key, the old key has to be deleted and the new one added to the map. We can create a map and add elements to it as follows:

```
// create a map
std::map<std::string, int> countries; // create empty map with a
                                      // string key and int value

// element access: Supports indexed access with no bounds
// checking and provides a range checked at() function
countries["USA"] = 1;     // USA country code 1
countries["DEU"] = 49;    // Germany country code 49
countries["CHN"] = 86;    // China country code 86
countries["IND"] = 91;    // India country code 91

countries.at("USA");      // country code = 1. bounds checked.
countries.at("JPN") = 81; // error. Out of bounds
```

When we use the [ ] operator to assign value to a key that does not exist in the map, it is added to the map and the specified value assigned to the key. Other functions available for a map are:

```
countries.erase(keyStr);   // erases element with
                           // key = keyStr
countries.find(keyStr);    // finds element with
                           // key = keyStr
countries.count(keyStr);   // returns count of elements
                           // with key = keyStr (0 or 1)

countries.max_size();      // maximum possible size for a map
countries.size();          // number of elements
countries.clear()          // erase all elements
countries.empty()          // true if the map has no elements
```

2.15.4 Iterators

Requires header file <iterator>.

Access to elements in a container is provided by using *iterators* that work with all STL containers. An iterator points to an element in a collection. The STL containers provide the following facilities to iterate through the elements in a container:

- An iterator of type container<type>::iterator

- A class member function **begin()** or the global function **std::begin()** that returns an iterator pointing to the first element of the container.

- The ++ operator that increments the iterator to move it forward one position in the container.

- The dereferencing operator * to access the value that the iterator points to.

- A class member function **end()** or the global function **std::end()** that returns an iterator pointing to one position past the last element of the container i.e. the iterator is pointing past the end of the container and the iterations should stop.

The types of iterators, in ascending order of capability, are: *input, output, forward, bidirectional* and *random access*. A **vector** provides random access iterators while a **map** provides bidirectional iterators.

Let us look at two examples of simple iterators:

```cpp
// create an int vector with 100 elements
std::vector<int> numbers(100);

// iterate over elements using member functions
int j = 0;
for(std::vector<int>::iterator i = numbers.begin();
    i != numbers.end();   // while not at end
    ++i)
    {
    *i = ++j; // assign values to elements
    }

// iterate over countries using global begin() and end()
j = 0;
for(auto i = std::begin(countries); // start
    i != std::end(countries);       // while not at end
    ++i)
    {
    i->second = ++j; // assign new values to elements
    }
```

We can create iterators in several ways as shown below:

```cpp
// creating different types of iterators
// iterators for forward traversal
auto iFrom = std::begin(numbers);
auto iUntil = std::end(numbers);
```

```
// iterators for reverse traversal
auto irFrom = std::rbegin(numbers);
auto irUntil = std::rend(numbers);

// iterators to insert elements in a container
auto iBackInsert = std::back_insert(numbers);   // at back
auto iFrontInsert = std::front_insert(numbers); // in front
```

Iterators are used as argument for many global functions defined in `<iterator>`:

```
// move within containers using iterators
std::next(iFrom, 3); // move forward 3 positions
std::prev(iFrom, 2); // move back 2 positions

// number of elements between irFrom and irUntil
auto diff = std::distance(irFrom, irUntil);
```

Many functions in the algorithms library (requires header file `<algorithm>`) also use iterators. For example, the `std::copy` function is used as follows:

```
// copy elements from one container to another using
// iterators
std::vector<int> target; // create empty vector

// Copy elements of numbers into target
// same as using target = numbers;
std::copy(iFrom,  // copy starting with this element
          iUntil, // copy until this element
          target.begin()); // add elements to target
                           // starting at this element
```

As we can see, iterators provide a consistent interface for sequential access of elements for containers in STL. They allow us to write generic for using containers.

Our average calculating program modified to use iterators is given below:

```
#include <cstdlib>
#include <iostream>
#include <vector>
#include <iterator>

// the main function
int main()
{
```

```cpp
short howMany,            // how many numbers to input
      numbersUsed = 0, // numbers used in calculations
      temp = 0;           // numbers used in calculations

double sum = 0.0,         // sum initialized to 0.0
      average = 0.0;   // average initialized to 0.0

std::vector<int> numbers;    // an empty vector

// input numbers into array
std::cout << "How many numbers? ";
std::cin >> howMany;

std::cout << std::endl
      << "To stop input at any time" << std::endl
      << "enter a number > 30,000\n" << std::endl;

for (int i = 0; i < howMany; ++i)
{
      std::cout << "Input number #" << i + 1 << ": ";
      std::cin >> temp;
      if (temp > 30000)
      {
            break;          // end input loop
      }
      numbers.push_back(temp);
}

// use vector iterator member functions to calculate average
for (auto num = numbers.begin();
      num != numbers.end();
      ++num)
{
      // num points to current element
      if (*num >= 10 && *num <= 20)
      {
            continue;          // go to top of loop
      }

      sum += *num;  // calculate sum
      numbersUsed++;          // increment count of numbers
}

average = sum / numbersUsed;
std::cout << std::endl << "Average of " << numbersUsed
```

```
        << " numbers is " << average
        << std::endl;
    return EXIT_SUCCESS;
}
```

The changes are highlighted in bold.

2.16 Dynamic Memory Allocation

In addition to memory allocated on the stack at compile time for declared variables, there is an additional pool of memory called the *heap* or *free store* available for the use in a program using *dynamic memory allocation* with the new and delete operators.

The new operator allocates memory and assigns its address to a specified pointer. If memory allocation fails, the result is a pointer with a value of nullptr. We should always check the value of the pointer after each allocation to ensure that memory allocation was successful. Memory can be allocated for any data type and the address stored in a pointer of the same data type. Examples of dynamic memory allocation are given below:

```
int *anInt = new int;      // allocate storage for one int
if(anInt == nullptr)
  {
   std::cout << "Error allocating memory" << std::endl;
  }

// allocates storage for 10 double numbers
double *numbers = new double[10];
if(numbers == nullptr)
   std::cout << "Error allocating memory" << std::endl;
```

Unlike static memory which is freed by the compiler when an object goes out of scope, dynamic memory must be freed explicitly by a program by using the delete operator as follows:

```
delete anInt;      // delete memory allocated for anInt
delete [] numbers; // deletes memory for numbers array
```

The brackets must be used to free up memory allocated for an array. The statement

```
delete numbers;
```

only frees up memory for the first element of the array. Memory allocated for the remaining elements of the array will not be freed.

The `delete` operator does not perform any operation if the pointer to allocated memory has the value `nullptr`. Therefore, it is safe to perform a `delete` operation on a block of memory for which the memory allocation failed.

2.17 Smart Pointers

Requires header file `<memory>`.

C++ provides *smart pointers* as an alternative to raw pointers for management of dynamic memory. Smart pointers are declared as local variables that exist on the stack and are destroyed automatically when they go out of scope. When a smart pointer is destroyed, it deletes the memory object managed by it. We do not have to explicitly delete the object using `delete`! This ensures that there are no memory leaks in our programs.

Some common properties of smart pointers are as follows:

1. The object managed by a smart pointer is accessed using the dereferencing operator * just like raw pointers.

2. Smart pointers provide a conversion to bool, so we can test a smart pointer to see if it manages an object or if it is empty:

    ```
    if(smartPointer)  // true if it manages an object
    ```

3. We can explicitly delete the object managed by a smart pointer as follows:

    ```
    smartPointer.reset();    // delete managed object
    smartPointer = nullptr; // delete managed object
    ```

4. The raw pointer of the managed object can be obtained as follows:

    ```
    smartPointer.get();
    ```

Smart pointers should be used instead of raw pointers to avoid memory leaks.

2.17.1 The unique_ptr

There is no overhead to using a `unique_ptr` as compared to raw pointers, so there is no impact on performance. We can create a `unique_ptr` pointer as shown below:

```
// create a pointer to manage an object of class aClass
```

```
std::unique_ptr<aClass> aPointer1(new aClass())

// create an empty pointer (value is nullptr)
std::unique_ptr<aClass> aPointer2;

// create a pointer to manage an int array of size 1000
std::unique_ptr<int[]> intPointer1(new int[1000])
```

A `unique_ptr` is the exclusive owner of the object managed by it and it cannot be copied or assigned to another `unique_ptr` by using its name (i.e. its lvalue):

```
// create a new pointer from an existing unique pointer
std::unique_ptr<int[]> intPointer3(intPointer1); // error

std::unique_ptr<int[]> intPointer4 = intPointer1;// error
```

We can, however, move the rvalue (i.e. the unnamed magnitude) of one `unique_ptr` to another using the `std:move` function as shown below:

```
// create intPointer3 by moving value of intPointer1
std::unique_ptr<int[]>
                intPointer3(std::move(intPointer1)); // OK

// assign intPointer3 to intPointer4 by moving its value
std::unique_ptr<int[]> intPointer4
                    = std::move(intPointer3); // OK
```

After the first statement, `intPointer3` points to the `int` array while `intPointer1` has a value of `nullptr`. After the second statement, `intPointer4` points to the `int` array while `intPointer3` has a value of `nullptr`. We are changing the owner of the managed object by transferring the managed object from one pointer to another. There is always only one owner of the managed object.

We can also explicitly assign an rvalue to a `unique_ptr`:

```
// assign rvalue to a unique pointer using new operator
std::unique_ptr<aClass> aPointer2;
aPointer2 = std::unique_ptr<aClass>(new aClass());

std::unique_ptr<aClass[]> anArray; // empty array pointer
anArray = std::unique_ptr<aClass[]>(new aClass[1000]);
```

We can use `unique_ptr` as a function parameter and as a function return type. However, you cannot pass a `unique_ptr` to a function by value because it involves making a copy of the pointer. It must be passed by reference as shown below:

```
// unique pointers as function arguments
```

```
void function1(std::unique_ptr<aClass> aPtr1);    // error
void function2(std::unique_ptr<aClass> &aPtr2);   // OK
void function3(const std::unique_ptr<aClass> &aPtr3); // OK
```

Function2 receives a non-constant reference to a unique_ptr and is free to change the ownership of the object managed by aPtr2. Function3 receives a constant reference to a unique_ptr and, therefore, cannot change the ownership of aPtr3.

```
// unique pointers as function return type
std::unique_ptr<aClass>& aClassPtr2(void); // return reference

std::unique_ptr<aClass> aClassPtr1(void)    // return value
{
    std::unique_ptr<aClass> aPointer(new myClass());

    return std::move(aPointer); // use move() to return rvalue
//    return aPointer;            // C++ implicitly uses move
//    return std::unique_ptr<aClass>(new aClass()); // new rvalue
}
```

Functions aClassPtr1 and aClassPtr2 both have to return the rvalue of a unique_ptr using any one of the three options shown in function aClassPtr1 above. Therefore, the return value of aClassPtr1 and aClassPtr2 can be assigned to a unique_ptr variable in a program that uses these functions.

The unique_ptr is the preferred method of managing pointers to allocated memory.

2.17.2 The shared_ptr

The shared_ptr smart pointer is used in situations where the same object is to be managed by several pointers. The shared_ptr keeps track of the number of pointers pointing to the managed object and the managed object is destroyed only when all pointers pointing to it are destroyed. Shared pointers are created as follows:

```
// create a pointer to manage int array of size 1000
std::shared_ptr<int[]>  intPointer1(new int[1000])

// add two members to intPointer1 group
std::unique_ptr<int[]> intPointer2(intPointer1);
std::unique_ptr<int[]> intPointer3 = intPointer1;
```

```
// convert intPointer2 to empty pointer. Use count for
// managed object will be decremented by 1
intPointer2 = nullptr;

// a new group to manage another int array of size 1000
std::shared_ptr<int[]> intPointer10(new int[1000])

// create an empty pointer (value is nullptr)
std::shared_ptr<int> intPointer20;
```

Shared pointers can be compared just like raw pointers: the comparison
operators compare the raw pointer of the managed object. There is an overhead to
using shared pointers. Therefore, they should be used only when their reference
counting capability is required.

2.18 Memory Allocation Example

Our average calculating program in the previous sections used static memory
allocation for the numbers array with a maximum size of 100. The maximum size of
the array is fixed in code. We can use dynamic memory allocation to remove this
limitation. We will modify the average calculating program to use dynamic memory
allocation for the numbers array with the size of the array input by the user:

```
#include <cstdlib>
#include <iostream>
#include <memory>

// the main function
int main()
{
    short howMany,          // how many numbers
          numbersUsed = 0;  // numbers used in average

    double sum = 0.0,
           average = 0.0;

    // input numbers into array
    std::cout << "How many numbers? ";
    std::cin  >> howMany;

    // use smart pointer for array storage
```

```cpp
    std::unique_ptr<double[]>
                numbers(new double[howMany]);
    if(numbers == nullptr)
      {
        std::cout << "Error allocating memory for array"
                << std::endl;
        return EXIT_FAILURE;          // end program
      }

    std::cout << std::endl
            << "To stop input at any time" << std::endl
            << "enter a number > 30,000\n" << std::endl;

    for(int i = 0; i < howMany; i++)   // input numbers
      {
        std::cout << "Input number #" << i+1 << ": ";
        std::cin  >> numbers[i];

        if(numbers[i] > 30000)
          {
            howMany = i;  // count of numbers in array
            break;          // end input loop
          }
      }

    // use numbers array to calculate average
    for(int i = 0; i < howMany; ++i)
      {
        if(numbers[i] >= 10 && numbers[i] <= 20)
          {
            continue;       // go to top of loop
          }

        sum += numbers[i]; // calculate sum
        numbersUsed++;     // increment count of numbers used
      }

    average = sum / numbersUsed;
    std::cout << std::endl << "Average of " << numbersUsed
            << " numbers is " << average
            << std::endl;
    return EXIT_SUCCESS;
}
```

The changes are highlighted in bold.

3   Functions

Functions group statements into named units that can be executed by *calling* the function. We have already seen the `main` function that every C++ program must have. A Function may be viewed as a module that performs a specific task. For example, a function to calculate speed of an object given the distance and time. A problem is decomposed into its component tasks and functions are developed to perform those tasks. This approach is called *functional decomposition*. A program is developed using these functions as modules. This programming paradigm is called *modular programming*.

3.1   Function Declaration and Definition

A function declaration specifies the calling interface of a function. Function definition provides the implementation of the function.

The structure of a *function definition* is as follows:

```
[Storage Class] [Return Type] Name(arguments list)
{
  // function body
}
```

The components of a function definition are:

- The optional *storage class* which determines the scope of the function. The valid values are `extern` or `static`. If a storage class is not given, `extern` is assumed. If the function has a storage class of `static`, it can only be directly invoked from within the same source file in which it is defined.

- The optional *return type* of the function. If a return type is not specified, the function has a return type of `int`. If the function does not return a value, the keyword `void` must be used as the return type.

- A function declarator, which provides the function name and, enclosed in parentheses following the name, a comma separated list of any parameters (and their types) that the function expects. These parameters are called the *formal arguments* of the function. If a function does not have any arguments, the parenthesis may be left empty or the keyword `void` may be specified.

- The *function body*, which contains data definitions and code. The body of a function appears between braces {} following the function declarator.

A function is called using the *call operator* (). If a function requires parameters, their values are placed inside the call operator in a comma separated list in the same order as in the list of formal arguments. The values in the function call are the *actual arguments*. The procedure is called *passing arguments* to a function.

A function must be declared before it is used. This declaration is called a *function prototype*. A function prototype specifies the calling interface of a function: the return type, the name and the formal parameters of the function. The prototype ends with a semicolon. You may declare a function as many times as you want, but all declarations for a given function must be the same. Function prototypes are usually specified in header files and included in the programs that use the function.

The example below shows a function named **speed** that calculates and returns speed using the values of distance and time passed as arguments:

```
#include <cstdlib>
#include <iostream>

// function prototype
double speed(double aDistance, double aTime);

// function definition
double speed(double aDistance, double aTime)
{
   double aSpeed;
   if(aTime > 0.0)
     {
      aSpeed = aDistance / aTime;
     }
   else
     {
      std::cout << "Value of time must be greater than 0"
               << std::endl;
      aSpeed = 0.0;
     }

   return aSpeed;
}

// the main function
int main(void)
```

```
{
    double distance,
           time;

    // input distance and time
    std::cout << "Distance? ";
    std::cin  >> distance;
    std::cout << "Time? ";
    std::cin  >> time;

    std::cout << "Speed = " << speed(distance, time)
              << std::endl;

    return EXIT_SUCCESS;
}
```

3.2 Return Values

A function must return a value using the return statement unless it has a return type of void. The return value can be a variable, a pointer, a reference or an expression that results in a value of the same type as the function return type. When returning pointers or references to variables, the variable should not be a local variable or object that will be destroyed when the function ends.

The following return statements show different ways of returning values to a caller:

```
return;            // Returns no value (optional)
return result;     // Returns the value of result
return 1;          // Returns the int value 1
return (x * x);    // Returns the value of x * x
```

References can be used as return types for functions. For example:

```
long& number()
{
    long *aNumber = new long; // allocate dynamic memory
    *aNumber = 100;           // assign value to aNumber
    return *aNumber;
}
```

The function number() can be used both as the value of and an alias for aNumber. This allows us to place the function call on the left side of assignment statements:

```
// function number() used to set i equal to aNumber
long i = number();

// function number() used as alias for aNumber
number() = 5;            // aNumber set equal to 5
```

A function can return only one value. If more than one value has to be returned, non-constant pointers or references to variables must be used as function parameters to return values. We will change the function **speed** above to return an error code indicating success or failure in the calculation of speed and use a function parameter to return the value of speed:

```cpp
#include <cstdlib>
#include <iostream>

// function prototype
int speed(double aDistance, double aTime,
              double *aSpeedPtr);

// function definition
int speed(double aDistance, double aTime,
              double *aSpeedPtr)              // for output
{
   if(aTime > 0.0)
      {
       *aSpeedPtr = aDistance / aTime;
       return EXIT_SUCCESS;
      }
   else
      {
       *aSpeedPtr = 0.0;
       return EXIT_FAILURE;
      }
}

// the main function
int main(void)
{
   double distance,
          time,
          aSpeed;

   // input distance and time
   std::cout << "Distance? ";
```

```
std::cin  >> distance;
std::cout << "Time? ";
std::cin  >> time;

if( speed(distance, time, &aSpeed) == EXIT_SUCCESS )
  {
    std::cout << "Speed = " << aSpeed << std::endl;
    return EXIT_SUCCESS;
  }
else
  {
    std::cout << "Error in calculation" << std::endl;
    return EXIT_FAILURE;
  }

}
```

The changes are highlighted in bold. The function speed uses a pointer to a double (aSpeedPtr) as a formal argument to output the value of speed. In the main function, we pass the address of double variable aSpeed as an actual argument. Inside the function, aSpeedPtr is dereferenced to assign the calculated value of speed to aSpeed.

3.3   Function Parameters

There are three ways to pass parameters to a function:

1. **Pass the variable itself**: The function gets its own copy of the variable and any changes made to the variable inside the function affect only the copy and not the original variable. This is called *passing by value*. When function parameters are large objects instead of built-in types, the overhead of passing by value is significant because the compiler has to create a copy of the passed object.

2. **Pass a pointer to the variable**: The function uses a pointer to the variable to access the original variable. The original variable may be changed inside the function. This method is very efficient for passing large objects as arguments.

3. **Pass a reference to the variable**: The function uses the reference to the variable to access the original variable. The original variable may be changed inside the function. The syntax for using the function is, however, the same as passing the variable by value.

The following example demonstrates the three methods of passing values:

```cpp
#include <cstdlib>
#include <iostream>

void function1(long i, long j)     // pass by value
{
    i += j;
}

void function 2(long* i, long* j)  // pass by pointer
{
    *i += *j;
}



void function 3(long& i, long& j)  // pass by reference
{
    i += j;
}

// the main function
int main(void)
{
    long a = 10;      // a is 10
    long b = 20;      // b is 20

    std::cout << "a = " << a << " and b = " << b
            << std::endl;

    function (a, b);  // call method1. a and b not changed.
    std::cout << "After Method 1: a = " << a
            << " and b = " << b << std::endl;

    function 2(&a, &b); // call method2. a changed to 30.
    std::cout << "After Method 2: a = " << a
            << " and b = " << b << std::endl;

    function (a, b);    // call method3. a changed to 50.
    std::cout << "After Method 3: a = " << a
            << " and b = " << b << std::endl;

    return EXIT_SUCCESS;
}
```

The calls to functions `function1` and `function3` look exactly the same. Similarly, the code for `function1` and `function3` is the same except for the declaration of formal arguments. However, the values of variables a and b cannot changed in `function1` because they are passed by value but may be changed in `function3` because they are passed by reference. The following guidelines should be followed for passing function arguments:

- Variables of built-in types that are not going to be modified inside the function should be passed by value.

- Large objects that are not going to be modified inside the function should be passed as references to `const` objects. This method combines the efficiency of passing by pointer with the safety of passing by value.

- Variables and large objects that are going to be modified inside the function should be passed using a pointer.

The example below modifies our average calculation program to use a function to calculate an average:

```cpp
#include <cstdlib>
#include <iostream>

// function to calculate an average
double average( short *count,
                const std::unique_ptr<double[]> &data )
{
   double sum = 0.0;
   short numbersUsed = 0;      // numbers used in average

   for(int i = 0; i < *count; ++i)
     {
       if(data[i] >= 10 && data[i] <= 20)
         {
           continue;         // go to top of loop
         }

     sum += data[i]; // calculate sum
     numbersUsed++;      // increment count of numbers used
     }

   *count = numbersUsed;
   return (sum / numbersUsed);
}
```

```cpp
// the main function
int main()
{
   short howMany;              // how many numbers
   double avg;                 // average

   // input numbers into array
   std::cout << "How many numbers? ";
   std::cin  >> howMany;

   // use smart pointer for array storage
   std::unique_ptr<double[]>
                numbers(new double[howMany]);
   if(numbers == nullptr)
     {
       std::cout << "Error allocating memory for array"
               << std::endl;
       return EXIT_FAILURE;            // end program
     }

   std::cout << std::endl
           << "To stop input at any time" << std::endl
           << "enter a number > 30,000\n" << std::endl;

   for(int i = 0; i < howMany; ++i)   // input numbers
     {
       std::cout << "Input number #" << i+1 << ": ";
       std::cin  >> numbers[i];

       if(numbers[i] > 30000)
         {
           howMany = i;  // count of numbers in array
           break;        // end loop and calculate average
         }
     }

   // use the function to calculate average
   avg = average(&howMany, numbers);

   // After call to function, howMany contains numbers
   // used in average calculation
   std::cout << "Average of " << howMany
           << " numbers is "
           << avg
           << std::endl;
```

```
    return EXIT_SUCCESS;
}
```

The changes are highlighted in bold. The average calculations only use the data in the numbers array but do not modify it any way. To ensure that the data in numbers array is not modified inside the function, we declare the numbers formal argument as a const.

3.4   Default Values for Parameters

We can set default values for function parameters. Parameters with default values must be the trailing arguments in the formal argument list. Once a default value has been specified for a parameter it cannot be redefined in another function declaration, even to the same value. However, you can add default values for parameters not specified in previous declarations as long as all trailing parameters have default values supplied in this or a previous declaration of the function. For example:

```
void x(int a = 1, int b = 1, int c);
// Error. Leading defaults

void x(int a, int b, int c = 1); // OK

void x(int a = 1, int b, int c);
// Error. Cannot add default for a because no default
// value defined for b. c already defaults to 3.

void x(int a, int b = 1, int c);
// OK. Adds default for b. c already defaults to 3.

void x(int a = 1, int b = 1, int c = 1);
// Error. Redefinition of defaults for b and c
```

When a function with default parameters is called with trailing parameters missing, the function declaration is checked for default values and the required default expressions are evaluated. All subsequent parameters must be defaulted once you start using default values. The order of evaluation of default expressions is undefined. Therefore, default expressions cannot use default values of other formal arguments of a function. For example:

```
void a(int a, int b = 1, int c = b);   // error. Cannot use b in
                                       // default expression for c
```

The argument c cannot be initialized with the value of the argument b because the value of b may not be known when it is assigned to c.

3.5   Overloaded Functions

You can overload a function by having multiple declarations of the same function name in the same scope. The declarations may differ in the type of and the number of arguments in the formal argument list. When you declare a function with the same name more than once in the same scope, the declarations of the function are interpreted by the compiler as follows:

- If the return type, argument types, and number of arguments of the two declarations are identical, the second declaration is considered a declaration of the same function as the first.

- If only the return types of the two function declarations differ, the second declaration is considered an error.

- If either the argument types or the number of arguments of the two declarations differ, the function is considered to be overloaded.

When an overloaded function is called, the correct function is selected by comparing the actual arguments with the types of and the number of the formal arguments to select the function to be called. The return types of functions are not compared. For example, a function named print can be overloaded as follows to display numbers and characters:

```
#include <cstdlib>
#include <iostream>

// overloaded print functions
void print(int i)          // prints integers
{
    std::cout << "An int: " << i << std::endl;
}

void print(double  f)      // prints doubles
{
    std::cout << "A double: " << f << std::endl;
}
```

```
void print(char* c)        // prints characters
{
   std::cout << " Characters: " << c << std::endl;
}

// the main function
int main()
{
   print(10);    // calls print(int) to print 10
   print(10.0);  // calls print(double) to print 10.0
   print("ten"); // calls print(char*) to print "ten"

   return EXIT_SUCCESS;
}
```

The main function is itself an example of an overloaded function. We have been using the main function in its simplest form. The return type of main may be int or void and the function may either take two parameters or no parameters. Valid overloaded declarations for main are as follows:

```
int  main(int argc, char *argv[])
int  main(void)
void main(int argc, char *argv[])
void main(void)
```

Although any name can be given to the input parameters in main, they are usually referred to as argc (argument count) and argv (argument vector). They are used as follows:

- The parameter argc is of type int and indicates how many arguments were entered on the command line, including the invocation name of the program.

- The parameter argv is a pointer to an array of null-terminated strings that has argc elements in the array:

  - The first element in argv is a pointer to the invocation name of the program that is being executed. If the name cannot be determined, it is set to NULL.

  - The subsequent elements in argv point to the arguments, if any, entered on the command line.

  - Regardless of the number of arguments entered on the command line, the element argv[argc] always contains NULL.

For example, if only the program name is entered on the command line, `argc` has a value of 1, `argv[0]` points to the program name and `argv[1]` contains `NULL`.

3.6   Standard C++ Library Functions

The standard C++ library provides many functions for use in our programs. Some useful functions for string and mathematical operations are listed below. You must include the header file `<cmath>` for mathematical functions and `<string>` for string functions. All these functions are in the `std` namespace, so they must be prefixed with `std::`.

- Mathematical functions: `log`, `log10`, `exp`, `pow`, `sqrt`, `abs`, `labs`, `fabs`, `cos`, `acos`, `sin`, `asin`, `tan`, `atan`, `ciel`, `floor`, `fmod`.

- String conversion functions: `stoi`, `stol`, `stoll`, `stoul`, `stoull`, `stof`, `stod`, `stold`, `to_string`, `to_wstring`. The functions with names starting with `sto` are used to convert from a string to a number (integer, long, long long, etc.) while the functions with names starting with `to_` convert numbers to a string.

Please consult the documentation for your C++ compiler to learn more about these functions.

4   Input and Output

4.1   Introduction

C++ uses streams defined in the Standard Template Library (STL) for input and output. A *stream* is sequence of characters that acts as a source or a destination for bytes of information. There are two types of streams:

1. Text streams contain printable characters and certain control characters organized into lines consisting of zero or more characters ending with a new-line (\n) character. A new-line character is not automatically appended to the end of a line. On output to a text stream, each new-line character is translated to a carriage-return character (\0d) followed by a line-feed (\0a) character. On input from a text stream, a carriage-return character followed by a line-feed character or a line-feed character alone is converted to a new-line character.

2. Binary streams are a sequence of characters or data. The data is not altered on input or on output. A new-line character in a binary stream is interpreted as a line-feed character.

The *iostream* library in the STL provides the facilities for standard input and output. We have already used iostream objects `std::cout, std::cin` and `std::endl` in our programs.

4.2   Iostreams

Iostreams present the same interface for input and output to standard I/O, to files and to an array of bytes in memory. Iostreams are accessed using the following methods:

- The *insertion operator* (`<<`): The characters are inserted into an output stream.

- The *extraction operator* (`>>`): The characters are extracted from an input stream.

- Methods of the iostream classes.

The >> and << operators have been defined for all built in C++ data types. User defined classes may also define custom insertion and extraction operators to provide a uniform way of performing input and output.

To improve system performance, Iostreams use *stream buffers* that act as temporary repositories for characters that are coming from the source of input or are being sent to the destination of output. Characters sent to an output stream are stored in the stream buffer and are sent to their destination when the buffer is full or when the buffer is *flushed*.

Iostreams use two primary base classes:

- The `streambuf` class to support stream buffers
- The `ios` class to manage the error state of a stream and the formatting of data.

4.3   Standard Input and Output

Requires header file `<iostream>`.

Standard input (`std::in`), standard output (`std::cout`), and standard error (`std::cerr`) are three pre-defined input and output streams available in C++. On most systems, `std::cin` accepts input from the keyboard while `std::cout` and `std::cerr` send output to the screen. We also have iostream *Manipulators* which are used to change the state of a stream. For example, `std::flush` which flushes the stream buffer and `std::endl` inserts a new line character into the stream and flushes the stream buffer. Let us look at an example:

```
#include <cstdlib>
#include <iostream>
#include <string>

int main()
{
    int i;
    double d;
    std::string str;

    // read from cin
    std::cout << "Input: integer double string"
             << std::endl;
    std::cin >> i >> d >> str;
```

```
    // display values read from input
    std::cout << "Values read from input: " << std::endl;
    std::cout << "i = " << i << std::endl;
    std::cout << "d = " << d << std::endl;
    std::cout << "string = " << str << std::endl;

    return EXIT_SUCCESS;
}
```

If the above code is run with the following input:

```
1 2.2 Worsel the dragon lensman
```

the output will be:

```
i = 1
d = 2.2
str = Worsel
```

By default, whitespace acts as a delimiter between values and is skipped when reading data. When reading input, the compiler reads in the characters representing the value and skips the delimiter after the value: the cursor is positioned at the first character of the data value after the delimiter. The next request for reading data starts from the current cursor position. In our example, the input works as follows:

1. The char '1' is read and the value of 1 is assigned to i. The next whitespace is skipped and the cursor is positioned at char '2'.

2. The characters '2.2' are read and the value of 2.2 is assigned to d. The next whitespace is skipped and the cursor is positioned at char 'W'.

3. The characters 'Worsel' are read and the value is assigned to str. The next whitespace is skipped and the cursor is positioned at char 't'.

String str contains only the first word Worsel because the space after the word is interpreted as a delimiter between values and not as a part of the string we want to read into str.

To input a string with embedded white spaces, we can use the global function std::getline(). For example, if we replace the code

```
std::cin >> i >> d >> str;
```

with the code

```
std::cin >> i >> d;              // cursor now positioned at 'W'
std::getline(std::cin, str);  // read all characters until \n
```

the string `str` will contain all characters between the current cursor position (the char 'W') and end of line marked by the new line character (\n) i.e. the entire string "`Worsel the dragon lensman`", including all embedded white space. The end-of-line delimiter is discarded and the cursor is positioned at the start of the next line. The primary use of the `std::getline()` function is to read one line of text input at a time and then parse the line for individual components.

To skip all data between the current cursor position and the end of the current line and to move the cursor to the start of the next line, we can use the iostream member function `std::ignore()` as follows:

```
// ignore all characters until \n (new line) is reached
std::cin.ignore(std::numeric_limits<std::streamsize>::max(),
          '\n');
```

The first argument is the maximum number of characters to ignore up to and including the character specified in second argument. The value `std::numeric_limits<std::streamsize>::max()` defined in header file `<limits>` is the max size of a stream.

We can display a value from any stream immediately by turning on automatic flushing for a stream using the `std::unitbuf` manipulator and disabling it using `std::nounitbuf`. The `std::cerr` stream already has auto flushing enabled so that error messages are displayed immediately.

```
std::cout << std::unitbuf << "Urgent message!\n"; // display now
std::cout << std::nounitbuf;  // turn off auto flushing
```

4.4   Stream Formatting

Requires header file `<iomanip>`.

The width, justification, precision, and other display properties of an iostreams are controlled by flags defined as enumerations in the `ios` class. The flags can be changed by one of the following methods:

1. Using manipulators defined in header file `<iomanip>`. The flags are set using the manipulator `setiosflags()` and cleared using the manipulator `resetiosflags()`. Two or more manipulators can be combined by using logical operators.

2. Using the iostream member functions. Function `setf()` is used to set a flag and `unsetf()` to clear it.

Except for the field width, once a flag is set, it persists until it is changed again. The formatting applies to both input and output streams.

4.4.1   Field Width

The field width used to display or read a data value can be changed by using the iostream member function `width()` or the manipulator `std::setw()`. The default field width is `0`: use as many characters as needed to display a field. The width setting is not persistent. The setting effects the only the input or output statement that follows the use of `width()` or `std::setw()`, after which the width reverts to the default setting. If the field width is not sufficient to display a data value, the width setting is ignored and the complete value is printed. There is no truncation of output.

```
// sets width to 10 for first output field after std::setw()
// width reverts to default value after printing "width 10"
// "Hello" is printed with default width
std::cout << std::setw(10) << "width 10" << "Hello"
          << std::endl;     // displays "  width 10Hello"

// the same result using member function
std::cout.width(10);
std::cout << "width 10" << "Hello" << std::endl;
```

The field width setting during input sets the number of characters that will be read for the next data value. The input will stop if whitespace is encountered before all the characters are read.

```
// sets width to 10 for first input field after std::setw()
// width reverts to default value after reading inp1
std::istringstream str("my width is 10");
std::string inp1, inp2;
str >> std::setw(10) >> inp1 >> inp2;
// on input, inp1 is "my" and inp2 is "width"
```

We can disable the skipping of whitespace during input by setting the `std::ios::skipws` flag or by using manipulators `std::skipws` and `std::noskipws` as shown below:

```
// sets width to 10 for first input field after std::setw()
// width reverts to default value after reading inp1
std::istringstream str("my width is 10");
```

```
std::string inp1, inp2;
str >> std::noskipws
    >> std::setw(10) >> inp1 // inp1 is "my". Cursor at ' '
                             // after 'y'
    >> inp2;                 // inp2 is ""
str >> std::skipws;          // restore skipping whitespace

// we can also use functions str.setf(std::ios::skipws)
// and str.unsetf(std::ios::skipws)to do the same thing
```

Note that the whitespace is still used as a delimiter but the delimiting space is not consumed automatically if `std::noskipws` is used. The `>>` operator for a `string` does not read whitespace so the cursor will not move any further until skipping whitespace is restored.

4.4.2   Justification

By default, all values are right justified within the field width with space as the fill character used for padding. To change the justification, use manipulators `std::left` and `std::right` or change the setting of the `ios::adjustfield` flag as shown below:

```
// Print right justified with width 20
std::cout.setf(std::ios::right, std::ios::adjustfield);
std::cout.width(20);
std::cout << "My width is 20"
          << std::endl;   // displays "      My width is 20"

// Print left justified with width 20
std::cout.setf(std::ios::left, std::ios::adjustfield);
std::cout << std::setw(20)
          << "My width is 20"
          << std::endl;   // displays "My width is 20      "
// restore default justification
std::cout.unsetf(std::ios::adjustfield);
```

We can change the fill character as shown below:

```
// change fill character to '.' using a manipulator
std::cout << std::setfill('.') >> std::setw(20)
          << "My width is 20"
          << std::endl;   // displays "......My width is 20"
```

```
// change fill character back to ' ' using member function
std::cout.fill(' ');
```

4.4.3   Displaying Numeric Values

The precision of a field determines the total number of digits that will be printed for both integers and floating point numbers. The default value of precision is 6.

The precision is set using the iostream member function `precision()` or the manipulator `std::setprecision()` as shown below:

```
// using default precision of 6
std::cout << 1234.56789    // displays 1234.56
          << 3456789       // displays 3456789. No truncation
          << std::endl;

// using precision of 4
std::cout.precision(4);
std::cout << 1234.56789    // displays 1235 (rounded up)
          << 3456789       // displays 3456789. No truncation
          << std::endl;

std::cout << std::setprecision(6) << std::endl;  // default
```

To always display a + sign before a positive number, use manipulators `std::showpos` and `std::noshowpos` or set the `ios::showpos` flag as shown below:

```
// Always show plus sign with integer
std::cout.setf(std::ios::showpos);
std::cout << 1234.56789    // displays +1234.56
          << 3456789       // displays +3456789. No truncation!
          << std::endl;

std::cout.unsetf(ios::showpos);    // restore default
```

Manipulators `std::oct`, `std::hex`, and `std::dec` are used to change the number base for displaying integers. The default mode for integer output is decimal. The octal and hex integers may be printed with an indication of their base by using the manipulators `std::showbase` and `std::noshowbase` or by setting the `ios::showbase` flag as shown below:

```
// printing integers using different bases
std::cout << "\n\n\nPrinting 10 using different bases"
```

```
         << std::dec << "\n as decimal = " << 10  // displays 10
         << std::oct << "\n as octal = "   << 10  // displays 12
         << std::hex << "\n as hex = "     << 10  // displays a
         << std::endl;

// can also use member functions for changing base:
// cout.setf(std::ios::dec, std::ios::basefield)
// cout.setf(std::ios::hex, std::ios::basefield)
// cout.setf(std::ios::oct, std::ios::basefield)

// printing the base along with the integer
std::cout.setf(std::ios::showbase);    // enable base display
std::cout << "\n\n\nPrinting 10 with base display"
         << std::dec << "\n as decimal = " << 10 // displays 10
         << std::oct << "\n as octal = " << 10    // displays 012
         << std::hex << "\n as hex = " << 10      // displays 0xa
         << std::endl;
std::cout.unsetf(std::ios::showbase); // disable showbase
std::cout << std::dec << std::endl;    // restore decimal
```

To print hexadecimal numbers in uppercase, use the following:

```
// Print hex numbers in uppercase
std::cout.setf(std::ios::uppercase);
std::cout << std::hex << "\n as hex = " << 10  // displays A
         << std::endl;
// Turn off uppercase printing
std::cout.unsetf(std::ios::uppercase);

// manipulators std::uppercase and std::nouppercase can
// also be used
```

The default method for displaying floating point numbers is compiler dependent. For example,

```
std::cout << 10 << std::endl;  // may display 10 or 10.0
```

To display a decimal point and trailing zeros for floating point numbers, use manipulators std::showpoint and std::noshowpoint or set the ios::showpoint flag as shown below:

```
// Default behavior
std::cout << 10.0              // displays 10
         << 0.000011           // displays 1.1e-005
         << 10000000.1         // displays 1e+007
         << std::endl;
```

```
// With ios::showpoint flag
std::cout.setf(std::ios::showpoint);
std::cout << 10.0            // displays 10.0000
          << 0.000011        // displays 1.10000e-005
          << 10000000.1      // displays 1.00000e+007
          << std::endl;
std::cout.unsetf(std::ios::showpoint);    // restore default
```

By default, floating point numbers are printed using fixed notation. However, if the decimal exponent of the number is less than -4 or it is greater than the precision, the output value is displayed in scientific notation. To force the use of a specified notation use manipulators `std::fixed`, `std::scientific`, `std::hexfloat` and `std::defaultfloat` or set the `ios::floatfield` flags as shown below:

```
// Default behavior
std::cout << 10.0            // displays 10
          << 0.000011        // displays 1.1e-005
          << 10000000.1      // displays 1e+007
          << std::endl;

// Using fixed notation
std::cout.setf(std::ios::fixed, std::ios::floatfield);
std::cout << 10.0            // displays 10.000000
          << 0.000011        // displays 0.000011
          << 10000000.1      // displays 10000000.100000
          << std::endl;

// Using scientific notation
std::cout.setf(std::ios::scientific,
               std::ios::floatfield);
std::cout << 10.0            // displays 1.000000e+001
          << 0.000011        // displays 1.100000e-005
          << 10000000.1      // displays 1.000000e+007
          << std::endl;

std::cout.unsetf(std::ios::floatfield); // restore default
```

If either `ios::fixed` or `ios::scientific` flags are set, the current value of precision is interpreted as the number of digits after the decimal point.

4.4.4　Displaying bool values

Values of type bool can be input from and output to a stream by setting the std::ios::boolalpha flag or using manipulators std::boolalpha and std::noboolalpha as shown below:

```
std::cout << "true: "  << true     // displays true: 1
          << "false: " << false    // displays false: 0
          << std::endl;
std::cout << std::boolalpha
          << "true: "  << true     // displays true: true
          << "false: " << false    // displays false: false
          << std::noboolalpha << std::endl;

// input using std::boolalpha
bool inp1, inp2;
std::istringstream str("true false");
str >> std::boolalpha >> inp1 >> inp2; // inputs true and false
```

4.5　File Input and Output

Requires header file <fstream>.

File I/O is supported by fstream, ofstream, and ifstream classes

- fstream classes are used for both input and output to the same file

- ofstream is used for output to files

- ifstream is used for input from files.

The files may be opened in text (the default) or binary mode.

4.5.1　Opening files

There are several different ways to open files:

```
// Open file for input
std::ifstream inpFile;
inpFile.open("fileName", mode);

std::ifstream inpFile("fileName", mode);

// Open file for output
std::ofstream outFile;
```

```
outFile.open("fileName", mode);

std::ofstream outFile("fileName", mode);

// Open file for input and output
std::fstream aFile;
aFile.open("fileName", mode);

std::fstream aFile("fileName", mode);
```

The **mode** flags determine the behavior of the file stream. The flags, defined as enumerations in the **ios** class, are as follows:

- **ios::in**: Open file for input. The file must exist (**ios::nocreate** is implied).

- **ios::out**: Open file for output. If the file already exists, the contents of the old file are discarded (**ios::trunc** is implied).

- **ios::app**: Open a file for appending (**ios::out** is implied). If the file already exists, contents of the old file are not discarded. Data that is written is appended to the end of the file.

- **ios::ate**: On open, position the cursor at the end of file. If the file is an output file and it already exists, contents of the old file are not discarded.

- **ios::nocreate**: The file must exist. On open, fail if the file does not exist.

- **ios::noreplace**: On open, fail if the file already exists. This flag is ignored if **ios::in** is set.

- **ios::trunc**: If the file already exists, discard the contents of the old file.

- **ios::binary**: Open the file in binary mode.

The flags may be combined to specify file **mode** as shown below:

```
// Open a new file for
// Opening fails if the file already exists.
std::ios::out | std::ios::noreplace

// Open an existing file for output.
// Contents of the existing file are deleted.
// Opening fails if file does not exist
std::ios::out | std::ios::nocreate
// (std::ios::trunc implied by ios::out)
```

```
// Open an existing file in output mode
// for appending data
std::ios::app | std::ios::nocreate
// (std::ios::out implied by ios::app)

// Open an existing file for output and position the
// cursor at the end of file
std::ios::out | std::ios::nocreate | std::ios::ate

// Open an existing file for input.
// Opening fails if file does not exist
std::ios::in
// (std::ios::nocreate implied by ios::in)

// Open an existing file for input in binary mode
std::ios::in | std::ios::binary
// (std::ios::nocreate implied by std::ios::in)
```

We can also open output files in binary mode by using `ios::binary` flag to the examples shown above.

4.5.2 Closing Files

The files may be closed using the `close()` member function as follows:

```
aFile.close();
```

The iostream destructor will close the file when the file object goes out of scope or is deleted.

4.5.3 Moving Within Files

The `<<` and `>>` operators perform their operations at the current position of the cursor in the stream. The position is specified in number of bytes from the beginning of file. This position changes as a result of I/O operations on the stream. The current position of the cursor is maintained in a *put pointer* for output streams and a *get pointer* for input streams. These pointer positions can be queried and changed using the following iostream member functions:

- `seekp()`: Moves the put pointer to the given location in file.
- `tellp()`: Gives the current location of the put pointer.

- seekg(): Moves the get pointer to the given location in file.

- tellg(): Gives the current location of the get pointer.

The pointer position can be set or queried by specifying a starting point for the operation using enumerations ios::beg, ios::cur, and ios::end defined in the ios class. Movement within a file accomplished as follows:

```cpp
// Open file for input
std::ifstream inpFile("fileName");

// Move to end of file and save current location
inpFile.seekg(0, ios::end);     // 0 bytes from end of file
std::streampos eof = inpFile.tellg();

// Use saved position to move backwards to
// the middle of file and save current position
inpFile.seekg(-eof/2, ios::end);
std::streampos middle = inpFile.tellg();

// Move to beginning of file
inpFile.seekg(0, ios::beg);     // 0 bytes from start of file

// Read a line of data at cursor location
char buffer[100];
inpFile.getline(buffer, 100);  // read line
std::cout << buffer << std::endl;  // print line

inpFile.close();                    // close the file
```

The cursor movement can be used to implement random access read and write operations.

4.5.4   Binary File Input and output

For binary files, the stream member functions read() and write() are used to read a specified number of bytes from a stream to or from a character buffer:

```cpp
read((char *)buffer, bytesToRead)
write((char *)buffer, bytesToWrite)
```

where buffer is a pointer to a character buffer.

The following code fragment demonstrates the use of the above functions:

```cpp
double array[10];
```

```
// fill array with data
...

// open file for binary output and save data in array
std::ofstream outFile("fileName",
                    std::ios::out | std::ios::binary);
outFile.write((char *)array, sizeof(array));
outFile.close();

// open file for binary input and read data to array
std::ifstream inpFile("fileName",
                    std::ios::in | std::ios::binary);
inpFile.read((char *)array, sizeof(array));
inpFile.close();
```

Functions `read()` and `write()` combined with the file movement functions can be used to implement random access read and write operations.

4.6   String Input and Output

Requires header file `<sstream>`.

Input and output to in-memory strings is a simple: convert a string into a string stream and then use standard stream functions to perform input and output.

4.6.1   Input String Streams

Input string streams are created as shown below:

```
// Input string streams

// Initialize string
string inpString = "50.0 Worsel the Dragon Lensman";

// open stream1 to read characters until null terminator
std::istringstream inStream(inpString);

// read from string inStream
double d;
string words;
inStream >> d >> words;
```

Reading from inStream will result in d = 50.0 and words = "Worsel".

4.6.2   Output String Streams

Output string streams are created and used as follows:

```
string store;
std::ostringstream aStream(store, ios::out);
```

The mode values are the same as for file streams. The string store must already be initialized with a null terminated string if mode ios::app is used: new characters are appended to the string starting at the null character.

A null terminator is not added after output to a string stream. It must be added explicitly using the manipulator std::ends. The code fragment:

```
// Output string stream

// Initialize character array with null terminated string
std::string store = "Old Characters:";

// open string stream for appending data to store
std::ostringstream aStream(store, std::ios::app);

// data to append to store
double d = 50.0;
std::string add = " Appended Characters";

// append data to store
aStream << d << add << std::ends;

aSream.close();
```

will result in store containing the null terminated string "Old Characters: 50 Appended Characters".

4.7   Redirecting Streams

The predefined streams std::cout, std::cin and std::cerr may be redirected to other streams. For example, the output sent to std::cout may be redirected to a file for appending data as follows:

```
std::ofstream outfile("logfile.txt",
```

```
                              ios::out | ios::app);
cout = outfile;
```

The output sent to cout will now be appended to the file logfile.txt.

4.8   Stream Buffer

The iostream member function rdbuf() returns a pointer to the stream buffer used by a stream. This pointer may be used to invoke the buffer functions directly. A common use of stream buffers is to dump the contents of one stream into another. For example, the statements

```
std::ifstream myFile("fileName", std::ios::in);
std::cout << myFile.rdbuf();   // move contents to cout
```

transfer the entire contents of a file to std::cout.

4.9   Stream Error Processing

Iostream objects such as std::cout maintain an internal error state. The objects may be used to check their state. For example, the if statement

```
if( ! std::cout )  // error
{
   ...
}
```

is true if std::cout is no usable and false if it is usable. In addition, several member functions are available for processing specific stream I/O errors:

1. good(): Returns true if there are no errors and the end-of-file flag is not set.

2. bad(): Returns true if there is an unrecoverable error and the integrity of the stream is compromised.

3. fail(): Returns true if there is either an unrecoverable error, a format conversion error or if the file is not found.

4. Operator !(): Using the operator ! is the same as using fail(): the expression if(!std::cout) is the same as if(std::cout.fail()).

5. eof(): Returns true if the end-of-file flag is set.

6. `clear()`: Changes the internal error state of the stream by clearing all error bits using the default parameters.

The following code segment demonstrates the use of the above functions to detect and handle file I/O errors:

```cpp
#include <cstdlib>
#include <iostream>
#include <fstream>

// the main function
int main()
{
    long buffer[100];

    // open file for input
    std::ifstream inpFile("fileName", std::ios::in);
    if( !inpFile )
      {
        std::cout << "Error opening input file"
                  << std::endl;
        return EXIT_FAILURE;
      }

    // read data into buffer array
    for(int i = 0;  i < 100;  i++)
      {
        inpFile >> buffer[i];
        if( inpFile.eof() )  // stop if at end of file
          {
            std::cout << "Reached end of file"
                      << std::endl;
            break;
          }

        if( inpFile.bad() )  // stop if unrecoverable error
          {
            std::cout << "Unrecoverable error"
                      << std::endl;
            inpFile.close();        // close file
            return EXIT_FAILURE;
          }

        if(inpFile.fail())          // formatting error
          {
```

```
            myFile.clear();        // clear error bits
            buffer[i] = 0.0;       // set value to 0.0
          }
      }

    inpFile.close();               // close file
    return EXIT_SUCCESS;
}
```

4.10 Input and Output using Iterators

We can use C++ STL iterators for input from and output to streams. Iterators for standard streams can be created as follows:

```
// iterators for standard streams
auto iCinInt = std::istream_iterator<int>(std::cin);
auto iStrInt = std::istream_iterator<int>(aStringStream);
auto iFileInt = std::istream_iterator<int>(aFileStream);
auto oCoutInt = std::ostream_iterator<int>(std::cout);
auto oStrInt = std::ostream_iterator<int>(aStringStream);
auto oFileInt = std::ostream_iterator<int>(aFileStream);
```

We can perform input and output using these iterators as shown below:

```
// input integers from cin into vector
std::vector<int> target; // create empty vector

std::copy(std::istream_iterator<int>(std::cin), // from cin
          std::istream_iterator<int>(), // until no ints
          std::back_insert(target)); // to target

// input integers from file into vector
std::ifstream aFile("integers.txt");
std::copy(std::istream_iterator<int>(aFile), // from file
          std::istream_iterator<int>(), // until no ints
          std::back_insert(target)); // to target

// input integers from string into vector
std::istringstream aStr("10 20 30 40 50");
std::copy(std::istream_iterator<int>(aStr), // from string
          std::istream_iterator<int>(), // until no ints
          std::back_insert(target)); // to target

// output integers from vector to cout
```

```
std::copy(std::begin(numbers), // from beginning of numbers
          std::end(numbers), // until the end of numbers
          std::ostream_iterator<int>(std::cout)); // to cout

// output integers from vector to file
std::ofstream aFile("integers.txt");
std::copy(std::begin(numbers), // from beginning of numbers
          std::end(numbers), // until the end of numbers
          std::ostream_iterator<int>(aFile)); // to cout

// output integers from vector to cout
std::istringstream aStr("10 20 30 40 50");
std::copy(std::begin(numbers), // from beginning of numbers
          std::end(numbers), // until the end of numbers
          std::istream_iterator<int>(aStr)); // to file
```

Input from and output to any stream can be done as shown above.

4.11 File I/O Example

We will now modify our average calculating program to read data from a text file and to save the output to a text file. The same file is used to save both input and output data. Our data is stored using the following format:

```
<<<<<<<<<< ------ File: data.txt
<<<<<<<<<< Created by Average Calculator
<<<<<<<<<< Created on: 08/10/2014 at 11:45:50
<<<<<<<<<< ------ Input Data
How many numbers          : 4
<<<<<<<<<< ------ List of numbers
Number                    : 10.0
Number                    : 20.0
Number                    : 30.0
Number                    : 40.0
<<<<<<<<<< ------ Output Data
Average                   : 35.0
```

The data file starts with a header section of four lines followed by sections for input and output separated by <<<<<<<<<< ------ xxx, where xxx is the section name. All lines starting with < are skipped

Each parameter is specified on one line as follows:

- Name of the parameter

- A colon (:) as a separator

- Value of the parameter

The name of the parameter is for documentation only. The program uses only the value specified after the colon.

To begin calculations, a data file containing only input data should be created manually by the user. The program reads the file, performs the calculations and writes both input and output data in the same file.

A function named **saveData** to save data in a file is given below:

```
// function to save data to a file
int saveData(const std::string &filename,
             const std::vector<double> &data,
             const double average)
{
  std::ofstream dataFile(filename.c_str(), std::ios::out );
  if(!dataFile)
    {
      std::cout << "Could not open file " << filename
                << " for writing data" << std::endl;
      return EXIT_FAILURE;
    }

  // C++ library functions to get local date and time
  char strDateTime[128];
  std::time_t now = time(NULL);
  std::strftime(strDateTime, sizeof(strDateTime),
                "%A %c", std::localtime(&now));

  dataFile.setf(std::ios::fixed, std::ios::floatfield);
  dataFile.precision(2);

  dataFile << "<<<<<<<<<< ------ Data File: " << filename
           << std::endl;
  dataFile << "<<<<<<<<<< Created by Average Calculator"
           << std::endl;
  dataFile << "<<<<<<<<<< Created on: " << strDateTime
           << std::endl;
  dataFile << "<<<<<<<<<< ------ Input Data"
           << std::endl;
  dataFile << "How Many Numbers      : "
           << data.size() << std::endl;
  dataFile << "<<<<<<<<<< ------ List of numbers"
           << std::endl;
```

```
   for(auto num = data.begin();
           num != data.end();
           ++num)
     {
      dataFile << "Number                    : "
              << *num << std::endl;
     }
  dataFile << "<<<<<<<<<<< ------ Output Data"
          << std::endl;
  dataFile << "Average                   : "
          << average << std::endl;

  dataFile.close();
  return EXIT_SUCCESS;
}
```

A function named `readData` to read data from a file is given below:

```
// function to read data from file
int readData(const std::string &filename,
           std::vector<double> &data)
{
  std::string buffer, label;

  std::ifstream dataFile(filename.c_str(), std::ios::in );
  if(!dataFile)
    {
     std::cout << "Could not open file " << filename
              << " for reading data" << std::endl;
     return EXIT_FAILURE;
    }

  // skip first 4 header lines
  std::getline(dataFile, buffer);
  std::getline(dataFile, buffer);
  std::getline(dataFile, buffer);
  std::getline(dataFile, buffer);

  // read count of numbers
  double count;
  // read line of data and create string stream
  std::getline(dataFile, buffer);
  std::stringstream aStream(buffer);
  // read label and value from string stream
  std::getline(aStream, label, ':');
```

```
        aStream >> count;

        // Skip list header
        std::getline(dataFile, buffer);

        // read count numbers
        double temp;
        for(int i = 0 ; i < count ; ++i)
          {
            // read line of data and create string stream
            std::getline(dataFile, buffer);
            std::stringstream aStream(buffer);
            // read label and value from string stream
            std::getline(aStream, label, ':');
            aStream >> temp;
            data.push_back(temp);
          }

        // Skip rest of file. We only need to read input data
        dataFile.close();
        return EXIT_SUCCESS;
}
```

We change the **average** function to use all available numbers to calculate the average value:

```
// function to calculate an average
double average( const std::vector<double> &data )
{
    double sum = 0.0;

    // num points to current element
    for(auto num = data.begin();
        num != data.end();
        ++num)
      {
        sum += *num; // calculate sum
      }

    return (sum / data.size());
}
```

The **main** function is changed to read data from and save data to a file:

```
#include <cstdlib>
#include <iostream>
```

```cpp
#include <fstream>
#include <sstream> // already includes <string>
#include <ctime>
#include <vector>

// the main function
int main()
{
    std::vector<double> numbers;        // empty vector
    double avg;                         // average
    std::string filename;               // name of data file

    // input name of data file
    std::cout << "Input name of data file: ";
    std::getline(std::cin, filename);

    // read data from file
    readData(filename, numbers);

    // calculate average
    avg = average(numbers);

    // save data in file
    saveData(filename, numbers, avg);

    return EXIT_SUCCESS;
}
```

The main function reads data from the specified file, performs the average calculations and saves both input and output data in the same file.

Part

OOPS!

5 Object Oriented Programming

What is Object Oriented Programming (OOP)? What are the characteristics of a programming language that make it object oriented? How is this paradigm different from the traditional modular programming based on functional decomposition? Why use it? We will examine these issues in this chapter.

5.1 Introduction

Software deals with both real world objects around us and abstract concepts from all fields of study. As software becomes more complex, it becomes difficult to relate the representation of objects and concepts using functional decomposition to the actual objects and concepts being modeled. It also becomes difficult and expensive to make changes because of intricate dependencies between functional modules. We need a representation system that will allow us to manage our software throughout its life cycle: conception, implementation, deployment and continuous product improvement. We need to consider the following:

- Real world objects have properties that describe them (their *state*) and they interact with other objects around them (their *behavior*). The two are related. The state of an object may influence its behavior and its actions may change its state. We need a mechanism to express objects such that the data needed to describe their state and the actions that define their behavior are kept together as a unit. A program will be composed of such units interacting with each other. These units relate directly to the objects being modeled, making the programs easy to understand and manage.

- We recognize relationships between objects around us. For example, Roses, Cherry Blossoms, Sun Flowers and Daises are all classified as flowers. All flowers share a common essence that make them flowers but, in addition, also have some special characteristics that make one type of flower different from another. We need a way to express such hierarchical relationships in our programs, where one class of objects can be represented as a special type of a more general class of objects.

- Complex objects in the real world are also assembled using other objects, i.e. by *composition*. We need to be able to do this in our programs.

- We often describe our actions involving similar objects in general terms but the outcome of our action is different for each object. For example, we say we are smelling flowers but when we smell a set of flowers, the smell of each type of flower is different. We want to be able to define general actions to deal with a class of objects but, at the same time, let the outcome express the qualities of the specific type of object being acted upon.

Object oriented languages provide us with the capability to do all this using the following features:

1. Classes and Objects are the fundamental building blocks for object oriented programming. They allow us to represent physical objects or abstract concepts and the relationships between them in programs in a manner that reduces the gap between reality and its representation. Combining data and functions that act on that data into a single object promotes clarity and localizes the problems inherent in code modification.

2. Inheritance enables us to reuse code by deriving new classes by extension of capabilities of existing classes.

3. Polymorphism lets us exploit the similarities between objects to define generic behavior for a class of objects while expressing the differences between specific objects of that class.

We will learn more about these features in this and subsequent chapters.

5.2   Fundamentals

The three main principles guiding the design and implementation of classes and objects in object-oriented programming are *abstraction*, *information hiding* and *encapsulation*. The objective of these principles is to develop robust software that reduces the cost of change relative to the benefits derived from the change.

5.2.1   Abstraction

An *abstraction* is a concise description of a physical object, an abstract concept or a procedure that can be stated without reference to the code used to implement the abstraction. An abstraction includes what is important or relevant for the application being designed and ignores what is not. In C++, an abstraction is represented by a *class*. A class becomes a new user defined data type, called an *abstract data type*. A class serves as a template or recipe for creating instances that may be used just like variables of built in C++ data types. An instance created from a class is called an *object* of the class. These objects exist only during program execution. Several objects of a class can exist simultaneously.

The state of an object is represented by variables (called *state variables* or *data members*) and its behavior by functions (called *methods* or *member functions*). These state variables and methods are called *members* of the class. All objects of the same class share the code used to implement the methods (common behavior) but have their own copy of the state variables (different state). The copies of state variables for an instance of a class are called *instance variables*.

Objects perform actions or have actions performed on them. Actions are performed by invoking the appropriate method. The actions may provide information about the object, change the state of the object, or perform actions based on the current state of the object that may or may not change the state of the object. There is a strong coupling between data and actions.

Let us consider an object we use every day: a chair. We want to develop a very simple simulation of a chair. The chairs in our simulation will only do the following:

```
Abstraction: Chair
State:       Color
             Style
             Weight capacity of the chair
             Broken? (weight on chair is more than its capacity)
Behavior:    1) Sit on the chair. Need weight of person.
             2) Get off the chair. Need weight of person
                that was sitting on the chair.
             3) Add more weight. Need weight to add.
             4) Remove weight. Need weight to remove.
             5) Ask how much weight on chair.
             6) Ask if chair is broken.
```

The above abstraction is far from a detailed simulation of a chair. We have only included the attributes we are interested in. All chairs in our program will have the same behavior but may have different colors, style and weight capacity.

The class used in our program to represent our abstraction of a chair will have state variables to represent color, style, current weight on chair, its weight capacity and its condition (whether or not it is broken). In addition, it will have methods to add weight, to sit on the chair, to remove weight, to get off the chair, to provide current weight on chair and to query if the chair is broken. The class may also have methods to initialize its data members, create new chair objects and perform other utility functions. Sometimes, performing an action requires additional information to complete the task. For example, the methods that adjust the current weight on the chair will require the weight being added to or removed from the chair. This input is supplied by using arguments for methods.

5.2.2   Information Hiding

Users of a class are interested primarily in its behavior – what the objects of a class can do. For them, a class is a "black-box" with a clearly defined *class interface* that states how the class may be used. Unlike users, designers of a class are interested in the details of how a class is implemented. As long as the class interface does not change, a program using our class will continue to work even if the details of the implementation are changed. In general, design details that are likely to change should be hidden from the users of a class. This is called *Information Hiding*.

The design details that should be kept hidden from the users include the following:

- The state of an object may be represented in many ways without changing the behavior of an object. For example, the color of a chair object could be stored as an integer, as a floating point number or as a set of RGB values. This is called *state representation ambiguity*. The data structures used to store the state of a class are most likely to change and should, therefore, be kept hidden.

- The methods that implement the behavior for a class should not expose the details of its state representation. Then, state representations can be changed easily at a later date without changing the methods of the class.

- The performance and reliability of programs can improved significantly as technology changes and new tools become available. The definition of a class interface should be based on user requirements and its implementation should hide the use of specific tools or technologies.

Changes in user requirements are eternal. We need to localize the impact of changes in code so that the cost of making such changes will be low. The code that implements the state of an object should be separated from the code that implements its class interface.

5.2.3   Encapsulation

Encapsulation is the language mechanism used to implement information hiding. C++ uses `public`, `private` and `protected` members to implement encapsulation. The members designated as `public` are accessible from outside the class. The members designated as `private` and `protected` cannot be accessed from outside the class. They may, however, be used by the other members of the class. The hidden design decisions of a class should always be made `private` members of the class. Most classes are designed with `private` state variables which cannot be accessed or changed except through functions called *accessor methods*. The methods that form the class interface are declared `public`. The methods of a class that are not a part of the class interface should be declared `protected` unless there is a specific requirement to declare them `private`.

5.2.4   Friends of the Class

C++ provides a mechanism for an external class or function that is not a member of your class to access private and protected members of your class. These classes and functions have to be declared as friends in the declaration of your class. The declaration can be placed anywhere in the class definition and is not affected by the access control keywords. Consider the following declarations in the definition of a class named `myClass`:

```
friend void aFriendFunction(myClass& arg);  // a friend function
friend aFriendClass;                         // a friend class
```

Function `aFriendFunction` can access all `private` and `protected` members of `myClass` using the reference to `myClass` (`arg`) specified as a parameter. The class `aFriendClass` can access all `private` and `protected` members of `myClass` but `myClass` cannot do the same with `aFriendClass`. It is a one-way friendship!

Friend functions are used in operator overloading discussed in Chapter 8. Any other use of friend functions should be avoided because they violate the information hiding requirement of object oriented programming.

5.3   Introducing Classes

In C++, a class declaration consists of the keyword **class** followed by the name of the class, followed by a class-body enclosed in braces, all terminated by a semicolon.

The body of a class definition consists of a definition of the state variables and methods of the class. The state variables of a class can be objects, pointers to objects or references to objects of built-in types or user defined classes. A user defined class has to be declared before its use. Usually, this means including the header file in which that class is defined. An alternative is to use a *forward declaration* (also called an *incomplete declaration*) to declare a class provided that:

- Only a pointer or a reference to that user defined class is used as a state variable.

- The user defined class is used as an argument type in a method.

- The user defined class is used as a return type in a method.

A forward declaration states only that the declared class exists. It says nothing about its structure. If structural details of a user defined class such as public members and size are also used, a forward declaration is not sufficient and the header file for that class has to be included. The structure of a class is given below:

```
#include <cstdlib>        // C++ standard library

// forward declaration of aUserClass is sufficient
Class aUserClass;         // only objects and references of this
                          // class are used in aClass below

#include "aUserClass1.h"  // required because size of this class
                          // is used in aClass below

Class aClass
{
// class body
private:
    int instanceVar1;
    int instanceVar2;
    int instanceVar3;
    aUserClass anObject;
    ...

protected:
```

```
        double method1(int arg);

public:
    aUserClass& method2(aUserClass1& arg, int sizeof(arg));
    ...

};
```

Methods of C++ classes are implemented like regular C++ functions. The main difference is the use of a scope resolution operator (::) to tell the compiler that the function name specified on the right side of the :: operator is a member of the class specified on the left side. For example:

```
void aClass::aMethod()
{
// body of the method
}
```

5.3.1   Creating Objects

We need a way to create objects (instances) of a class. A class uses special methods (called *factory methods*) to create its instances. In C++, factory methods are called *constructors*. Using a constructor is the only way to create an object. Therefore, constructors are used to ensure that all state variables and any other resources required by an object are properly initialized. The name of a constructor is the same as the name of the class. A constructor has no return type, not even **void**. A constructor may be declared **public** or **private**. A class may have several constructors as long as their input parameters are of different types i.e. the constructor can be overloaded.

A constructor without any input parameters is called the *default constructor*. A default constructor is used by the C++ compiler to initialize variables and arrays of a class. If no default constructor is available, variables and arrays of that class cannot be initialized without an explicit call to one of its constructors with parameters. Therefore, you should always define a default constructor for your classes. If a class does not define any constructor, the C++ compiler creates a default constructor for the class. However, if a class defines at least one constructor with parameters but does not define a default constructor, the compiler will not create a default constructor for the class. If a class defines a constructor with parameters which has default values specified for all its parameters, the compiler will use it as a default constructor because it can be invoked without arguments.

While constructors may also be implemented as regular functions, C++ provides facilities that result in more efficient code for constructors. One such facility is an *initialization list*. State variables should be initialized in the initialization list in the same order as they are declared in the class definition. State variables of built-in C++ data types may also be initialized efficiently in the body of the constructor using assignment statements. Arrays, however, can only be initialized using the assignment statements in the body of the constructor. Both assignment statements and an initialization list may be used in the same constructor.

```
// default constructor with an initialization list
aClass :: aClass()
        : instanceVar1(10),   // instanceVar1 = 10
        : instanceVar2(20),   // instanceVar2 = 20
        : instanceVar3(30),   // instanceVar3 = 30
{
}
```

We can call one constructor of a class from another constructor of the same class. This facility can be used to streamline the constructors of a class by using *delegating constructors* as shown below:

```
// default constructor delegates the job of creating an
// object to the constructor with parameters which is called
// the target constructor
aClass :: aClass()
        : aClass(10, 20)   // call the target constructor
{
}

// all initialization code in this constructor.
// Other constructors of the class call it with specific
// parameter values to create instances of the class
aClass :: aClass(int param1, int param2)
        : instanceVar1(param1),   // instanceVar1 = param1
        : instanceVar2(param2),   // instanceVar2 = param2
        : instanceVar3(30),       // instanceVar3 = 30
{
    std::cout << "Contructed an object" << std::endl;
}
```

All instance initialization code is in the constructor with parameters. It is called the *target constructor*. The default constructor *delegates* the task of creating an object to the target constructor by calling it to create an object with the specified default parameter values.

5.3.2   The copy constructor

We have used initialization at declaration for built-in C++ data types. We can do the same thing for objects of our own classes. Let us examine the following four statements:

```
aClass var1, var2;    // create aClass objects var1 and var2
aClass var3(var1);    // create var3 by copying var1
aClass var4 = var1;   // declare and initialize var4 with var1
var2 = var1;          // assign var1 to var2
```

The first statement creates two new **aClass** objects using the default constructor for the class.

The second statement creates a new **aClass** object named **var3** by copying an existing object **var1** of the same class using a constructor that takes another **aClass** object as an argument. The form of the constructor is as follows:

```
aClass(const aClass &source);
```

This constructor is called a *copy constructor*. The constructor copies a specified object into a new object as it is created. If you do not define a copy constructor for your class, the C++ compiler will generate one for you. The compiler generated copy constructor copies the values of all instance variables, including pointers, from the source object into the new object being created. This is called making a *shallow copy*.

For classes with pointer data members, the value stored in the pointer will be copied and the pointer members in both the source object and its copy will point to the same blocks of memory. However, we want the new object to have its own blocks of memory which are filled with the same content as the source object. To do that we must provide our own copy constructor which:

- Allocates memory for each pointer member in the new object.
- Copies data pointed to by pointers in the source object into the corresponding memory blocks in the new object.

This copy process is called making a *deep copy*.

The third and fourth statements both appear to copy `var1` to another `aClass` object using the assignment operator. However, their execution is completely different.

The third statement first creates a new object named `var4` and then copies the contents of `var1` into `var4`. Because the process involves creation of a new object, it is done using the copy constructor.

The fourth statement assigns `var1` to an existing object `var4` (copy by assignment). Copy by assignment does not involve creation of a new object and the assignment operator is used to make the copy. If you do not define an assignment operator for your class, the C++ compiler will generate one for you. The compiler generated assignment operator makes a shallow copy of the source object. For classes having pointer data members, we must provide our own assignment operator that makes a deep copy. We will look at operator overloading in a later chapter.

We should implement a copy constructor and override the assignment operators for all classes having pointers as data members.

Let us consider a class named `MarksList` which uses a `vector<double>` to store marks for all students in a course:

```cpp
class MarksList
{
 private:
   short numberOfStudents;
   std::vector<double> marks;          // vector to store marks

 public:
   MarksList(short students = 100);     // constructor
   MarksList(const MarksList &aList);   // copy constructor
   ~MarksList();                        // destructor
   short students() const;
   double getMarks(short studentID) const;
};
```

Because the `MarksList` class uses a pointer member, we must provide our own copy constructor for the class. The code for the constructors and the destructor is given below:

```cpp
MarksList::MarksList(short students)
{
    numberOfStudents = students;
```

```
    // set size of vector
    marks.resize(students);

    // fill marks with random numbers between 0 and 100
    for(int i = 0; i < marks.size(); ++i)
        marks[i] = rand() % 100 + 1;
}

// copy constructor
MarksList::MarksList(const MarksList &aList)
{
    // copy data from aList to this list
    numberOfStudents = aList.students();

     marks.resize(numberOfStudents);
    // copy array from aList into marks
    for(int i = 0; i < marks.size(); ++i)
        marks[i] = aList.getMarks(i);
}

MarksList::~MarksList()
{
}

short MarksList::students() const
{
    return numberOfStudents;
}

double MarksList::getMarks(short studentID) const
{
    return marks[studentID];
}
```

The copy constructor first allocates memory for the marks array in the new
object and then copies the contents of the marks array from the source object to
the marks array in the new object. The copy process now works correctly. We will
look at overriding assignment operators in Chapter 8.

5.3.3 Destroying Objects

The C++ run-time always calls a method called a *destructor* when an object is destroyed. A class can have only one destructor. The name of the destructor is the same as the name of the class preceded by a ~. A destructor has no return type, not even **void,** and it does not take any parameters. A destructor is used to ensure that memory and other dynamic resources created and used by an object are released properly. You should always define a destructor for your class, even if it does nothing.

5.3.4 Pointers and References to Objects

We can declare and use pointers and references to objects of user defined classes just like we can for C++ built-in types. For example:

```
aClass *var1 = new aClass();   // allocate memory using new
                               // operator and use default
                               // constructor to initialize
aClass *var2 = new aClass(4, 0); // uses constructor with
                               // parameters to initialize
const aClass &var3 = *var1     // constant reference to var1
```

The first two statements do the following:

- Use the **new** operator to allocate memory required to store an object of class **aClass.**

- Assign the address of the object to a pointer of type **aClass.**

- Initialize the newly created object using a constructor.

C++ provides a *member selection operator*, ->, to dereference pointers to objects to access the public members of a class. For example, we can access the public instance variables and methods by dereferencing the pointer **var1** or by using the reference **var3** as shown below:

```
(*var1).method1(50.0);  // by dereferencing pointer var1
(*var1).method2();      // by dereferencing pointer var1

var1->method1(50.0);    // by member selection with var1
var1->method2();        // by member selection with var1

var3.method1(50.0);     // using reference var3
var3.method2();         // using reference var3
```

5.3.5   The this Pointer

Objects contain instance variables and methods. Within an object, C++ provides access to the address of the object itself using a pointer named **this**. The C++ compiler implicitly uses the **this** pointer to access instance variables and methods. We can also explicitly use the **this** pointer to access the instance variables and member functions of an object. For example, an instance variable in an object may be assigned a value using the syntax:

```
instanceVariable = x + y;          // implicit use of this pointer

this->instanceVariable = x + y; // explicit use of this pointer
```

The **this** pointer is also passed as a hidden argument when calling a method and is, therefore, available inside the called method:

```
// calling a member function
anObject.aMethod(arg);

// the hidden first argument passing the address of the object
anObject.aMethod(&anObject, arg);
```

The primary use of the **this** pointer is to return the current object, a pointer to the current object or a reference to the current object from a method.

5.3.6   Arrays of Objects

We can also create arrays of objects just like arrays of built-in types. The statement:

```
aClass *aClassArray = new aClass[20];
```

creates an array of 20 objects of class **aClass** initialized using the default constructor or a constructor with all arguments having default values.

5.3.7   const Objects

As in the case of built-in data types, we can also create **const** objects of our class:

```
const aClass anObject;
```

The values of instance variables of a `const` object cannot be changed. Therefore, the compiler will not let you invoke any public method of a `const` object because the compiler assumes that all methods of a class are capable of changing the values of instance variables of the object. Most classes have methods that only use or return values of instance variables but do not modify their values. We should, therefore, be able to call these methods even from a `const` object. C++ provides a mechanism to tell the compiler which methods are safe to use with `const` objects. We must specify the `const` keyword in the method definition as shown below:

```
double method1() const;            // safe for const object
double method2(double arg1) const; // safe for const object
double method3();                  // not safe for const object
```

Methods `method1` and `method2` may be called from `const` objects of class `aClass`. The `const` keyword becomes a part of the signature of the class and must also be used in the implementation of the class:

```
double aClass::method1() const
{
    // do something
    return aDouble;
}
```

It is good practice to declare `const` methods because it makes a class more usable.

5.4 Implementing the Chair Class

A `Chair` class is implemented using two files: the `Chair` class definition in a header file named `chair.h` and its implementation in a file named `chair.cpp`. We have to include `chair.h` in any program that uses the `Chair` class.

5.4.1 Class Definition

The code below gives the definition of a `Chair` class based on the chair abstraction discussed above:

```
// file: chair.h
// chair class definition
```

```cpp
#ifndef CHAIR_H
#define CHAIR_H

class Chair
{
public:
    enum class styles { basic, modern, traditional };
    enum class colors { black, white, red, green, blue };

private:        // all state variables are made private
    colors  acolor;        // color of a chair
    styles  astyle;        // style of a chair
    bool    broken;        // is the chair broken?
    double  currentLoad;   // current total weight on chair
    double  maxWeight;     // weight capacity of the chair
    double  personWeight;  // weight of person sitting
                           // on chair. No person = -1
    double  addedWeight;   // non person weight added to chair.

 protected:
    double  setCurrentWeight();

 public:
    // constructors and destructor
    Chair();
    Chair(colors aColor, styles aStyle);
// Chair(const Chair &aChair); // copy constructor
    ~Chair();                        // destructor

    // methods
    double  sit(double weightOfPerson);    // sit on chair
    double  getOff();                       // get off the chair
    double  addWeight(double aWeight);     // add weight
    double  removeWeight(double aWeight); // remove weight
    double  currentWeight()const;          // weight on chair
    bool    isBroken() const;              // true if broken
    bool    isSitting() const;             // true if person seated
    void clear();                          // set weight to 0.0
    void refurbish();        // make the chair new again!

    // accessor methods for private state variables
    colors color() const;
    Chair& setColor(colors aColor);
    styles style() const;
    Chair& setStyle(styles aStyle);
```

```
    double capacity() const;
    Chair& setCapacity(double limit);
};

#endif  // CHAIR_H
```

Header file `chair.h` uses a *define guard* to protect against multiple inclusions. The first time we include this file, the constant `CHAIR_H` is not defined and `#if` directive evaluates to `true`. Inside the `if` block, the constant `CHAIR_H` is defined and contents of the file are included in the program. If this file is included again, the constant `CHAIR_H` is already defined and the `#if` directive evaluates to `false`. Therefore, the contents of the file are not included.

The class members are as follows:

- **Enumerations**: Enums `colors` and `styles` are defined to provide admissible values for chair colors and styles.

- **Private state variables**: All state variables are declared `private`, with public accessor methods to get and set their values. The weight of a person sitting on the chair is tracked separately from the weight of other articles put on the chair. The value of `personWeight` is `-1.0` if no one is sitting on the chair. Otherwise, its value is the weight of the person sitting on the chair.

- **Protected members**: The method `setCurrentWeight` is used by other methods to calculate the total weight on chair but is not a part of the public interface of the class.

- **Constructors**: The class has two constructors: a default constructor and a constructor with parameters. A copy constructor is not defined for the `Chair` class because it does not use any pointer members. The default copy constructor provided by the compiler will be used.

- **Destructor**: The class has a destructor that does nothing.

- **Public Members**: The public interface includes the following:
  - Accessor methods for private data members
  - Methods to sit on the chair, to get off the chair, put additional weight on the chair and to take weight off the chair.
  - Methods `currentWeight`, `isBroken` and `isSitting` to query the state of the chair.

The class interface of the `Chair` class is the `public` members of the class: a contract that states how the class may be used. As long as the class interface is not changed in any way, the programs using the class will keep working as before even if the private members and the details of the class implementation are changed.

5.4.2 Implementing Constructors and Destructor

The two constructors for the Chair class may be implemented as follows:

```
Chair :: Chair()
        : Chair(colors::black, styles::basic)
{
    std::cout << "Default Constructor: Chair" << std::endl;
}

Chair :: Chair(colors aColor, styles aStyle)
        : acolor(aColor),        // set color to aColor
          astyle(aStyle),        // set style to aStyle
          broken(false),         // set broken to false
          currentLoad(0.0),      // set currentLoad to 0.0
          maxWeight(100.0),      // set weight capacity to 100.0
          personWeight(-1.0),    // set person weight to -1.0
          addedWeight(0.0)       // set added weight to 0.0
{
    std::cout << "Constructing a Chair object" << std::endl;
}
```

Note the appending of the class name to the method name using the notation Chair::Chair and the use of an initialization list to set initial values for data members of the chair class. The second constructor may also be implemented using assignment statements as follows:

```
Chair :: Chair(colors aColor, styles aStyle)
{
    acolor = aColor;
    astyle = aStyle;
    broken = false;         // set broken to false
    currentLoad = 0.0;      // set currentLoad to 0.0
    maxWeight = 100.0;      // set weight capacity to 100.0
    personWeight = -1.0;    // set person weight to -1.0
    addedWeight = 0.0;      // set added weight to 0.0

    std::cout << "Constructing a Chair object" << std::endl;
}
```

The two definitions of the second constructor are equivalent.

The destructor for the chair class is shown below:

```
Chair::~Chair()
{
    std::cout << "Destroying a Chair object" << std::endl;
}
```

5.4.3   Implementing Other Methods

The remaining methods for the Chair class are implemented as shown below:

```
double Chair::sit(double weightOfPerson)
{
    if(broken)      // cannot sit on a broken chair
    {
        std::cout << "Cannot sit on a broken chair!" << std::endl;
        return currentLoad;
    }

    if(!(personWeight < 0.0)) // Someone sitting on chair
    {
        std::cout << "This chair is taken!" << std::endl;
        return currentLoad;
    }

    personWeight = weightOfPerson;
    return setCurrentWeight();
}

double Chair::addWeight(double aWeight)
{
    if(broken)  // do not add weight to a broken chair
    {
        std::cout << "Cannot add weight to a broken chair!"
                  << std::endl;
        return currentLoad;
    }

    addedWeight += aWeight;
    return setCurrentWeight();
}

double Chair::getOff()
{
```

```
   if(broken)
   {
      std::cout << "The chair is broken!" << std::endl;
      return currentLoad;
   }

   if(personWeight < 0.0)
   {
      std::cout << "No one is sitting on the chair!"
                << std::endl;
      return currentLoad;
   }

   personWeight = -1.0;
   return setCurrentWeight();
 }

double Chair::removeWeight(double aWeight)
{
   if(broken)
   {
      std::cout << "The chair is broken!" << std::endl;
      return currentLoad;
   }

   addedWeight -= aWeight;
   if(addedWeight < 0.0)
   {
    addedWeight = 0.0;
   }

   return setCurrentWeight();
}

double Chair::currentWeight() const
{
   return currentLoad;
}

double Chair::setCurrentWeight()
{
   if( personWeight < 0.0 )
   {
   currentLoad = addedWeight;
   }
```

```
        else
        {
        currentLoad = personWeight + addedWeight;
        }
        if(currentLoad > maxWeight)
          {
            broken = true;
            std::cout << "Weight more than capacity. The chair broke!"
                      << std::endl;
          }
        return currentLoad;
}

bool Chair::isBroken() const
{
        return broken;
}

bool Chair::isSitting() const
{
        if(personWeight < 0.0)
            return false;
        else
            return true;
}

void Chair::clear()
{
        currentLoad = 0.0;
}

void Chair::refurbish()
{
        acolor = colors::black;
        astyle = styles::basic;
        broken = false;          // set broken to false
        currentLoad = 0.0;       // set currentLoad to 0.0
        maxWeight = 100.0;       // set weight capacity to 100.0
        personWeight = -1.0;     // set weight of last sit to -1.0
        addedWeight = 0.0;       // set added weight to 0.0
}

Chair::colors Chair::color() const
{
        return acolor;
```

```
}

Chair& Chair::setColor(colors aColor)
{
    acolor = aColor;
    return *this;
}

Chair::styles Chair::style() const
{
    return astyle;
}

Chair& Chair::setStyle(styles aStyle)
{
    astyle = aStyle;
    return *this;
}

double Chair::capacity()const
{
    return maxWeight;
}

Chair& Chair::setCapacity(double limit)
{
    maxWeight = limit;
    return *this
}
```

5.5   Using the Chair Class

The main function below shows how to use the Chair class:

```
#include <iostream>
#include "chair.h"

int main()
{
    Chair aChair(Chair::colors::red, Chair::styles::modern);
    aChair.sit(50.0);        // person of weight 50 sits on chair
    aChair.addWeight(25.0); // add 25 additional weight
    std::cout << std::endl << "Properties of aChair:"
```

```
            << std::endl
            << "Weight : " << aChair.currentWeight()
            << std::endl
            << "Color : " << (int)aChair.color() << std::endl
            << "Style : " << (int)aChair.style()
            << std::endl  << std::endl;

    Chair chair2;        // use default constructor
    chair2.sit(150.0);   // the chair will break. Capacity = 100.0
    chair2.refurbish();  // make the chair new again

    // Chaining of function calls.
    // Chain breaks at clear() because it returns void
    // and not Chair&
    chair2.setColor(Chair::colors::green)
          .setStyle(Chair::styles::modern)
          .clear();
    std::cout << std::endl << "Properties of Chair2:"
            << std::endl
            << "Weight : " << chair2.currentWeight()
            << std::endl
            << "Color : " << (int)chair2.color() << std::endl
            << "Style : " << (int)chair2.style()
            << std::endl  << std::endl;

    return EXIT_SUCCESS;
}
```

The setColor(), setStyle() and setCapacity() methods return a reference to the Chair object. Therefore, they can be called in a chain as shown above. An interface that allows chaining of a sequence of operations is called a *fluent interface*.

The main function will not have to be changed unless the public class interface of the Chair class is changed.

5.6   Adding to the Chair Class

When multiple instances of a class are created, each instance has its own copy of the state variables. Often, we want to track characteristics (attributes) of the class as a whole. For example, for our Chair class we may want to track the average weight of persons sitting on our chairs or the total volume of material used to make all the chairs. These attributes are calculated based on the use of or the properties of all the chairs objects we have created. They do not belong to a specific chair but to the Chair class. These attributes exist even if we do not create any Chair objects.

5.6.1 Class Variables and Methods

We want to create state variables that only have one copy that is accessible by all instances of the class. The shared state variables are called *class variables* because they belong to the class as a whole and not to a particular instance of the class. The class variables describe the state of a class just as instance variables describe the state of an object.

A class variable is declared using the keyword **static**. Static data members must be initialized in the class implementation file outside the body of the class. They cannot be initialized in a constructor because the value will then be initialized every time an instance is created. Public class variables can be accessed directly by programs using the class name:

```
aClass.staticVar  // accessing public static class variable
```

Private class variables can only be accessed using static methods called *class methods*. Static methods can be accessed directly by programs using the class name:

```
aClass.staticMethod()  // calling a static method
```

Class variables and methods can be used even if no instances of the class exist. Class methods can only access other class variables and class methods. They cannot access instance variables of an object of the class or any non-static methods of the class.

5.6.2 A Better Chair

We will now add two new capabilities to our Chair class:

- **Track the number of active chair objects in our program**: We could setup a counter in the **main** program that is incremented every time a chair object is created in our program and decremented every time a chair object is destroyed. However, it is difficult to do so in a complex program because we cannot always know when or where an object is being destroyed. The best method is to define a class variable for the Chair class to use as a counter to track the number of chair objects created by our program. The best place to increment the chair count is in the constructors because a constructor is called whenever a `Chair` object is created. The best place to decrement the chair count is in the destructor because the destructor is called whenever a `Chair` object is destroyed. This counting process is automatic and error free. We will provide a public class method to access the chair count.

- **Calculate the average weight of persons sitting on chairs**: We will need to define two class variables for this: one to store the cumulative weight of persons sitting on our chairs and another to count the number of persons. The weight of a person sitting on a chair is added to the cumulative weight when the `sit()` method is called and the person count is incremented by 1. We will calculate and return the average weight using a public class method.

The definition of the modified `Chair` class is given below:

```cpp
// file: newchair.h
// chair class definition
#ifndef NEWCHAIR_H
#define NEWCHAIR_H

class Chair
{
public:
    enum class styles { basic, modern, traditional };
    enum class colors { black, white, red, green, blue };

private:        // all state and class variables are made private
    static double cumulativeWeight;
    static long numberOfPersons;
    static long chairCounter;

    colors  acolor;        // color of a chair
    styles  astyle;        // style of a chair
    bool    broken;        // is the chair broken?
    double  currentLoad;   // current total weight on chair
    double  maxWeight;     // weight capacity of the chair
    double  personWeight;  // weight of person sitting
                           // on chair. No person = -1
    double  addedWeight;   // non person weight added to chair.

protected:
    double  setCurrentWeight();
```

```
  public:
    // constructors and destructor
    Chair();
    Chair(colors aColor, styles aStyle);
//  Chair(const Chair &aChair); // copy constructor
    ~Chair();                    // destructor

    // methods
    static double averageWeight();  // calculate average weight
    static long activeChairs();     // calculate average weight

    double  sit(double weightOfPerson);    // sit on chair
    double  getOff();                      // get off the chair
    double  addWeight(double aWeight);     // add weight
    double  removeWeight(double aWeight);  // remove weight
    double  currentWeight()const;          // weight on chair
    bool    isBroken() const;              // true if broken
    bool    isSitting() const;             // true if person seated
    void clear();                          // set weight to 0.0
    void refurbish();        // make the chair new again!

    // accessor methods for private state and class variables
    colors color() const;
    Chair& setColor(colors aColor);
    styles style() const;
    Chair& setStyle(styles aStyle);
    double capacity() const;
    Chair& setCapacity(double limit);
};

#endif  // NEWCHAIR_H
```

The additions are highlighted in bold.

Changes in the class implementation are as follows:

- The class variables are initialized in the implementation file outside the body of the class.

- The constructors and the destructor for the Chair class are modified to increment and decrement the chairCounter.

- Class function activeChairs() is implemented.

- Member function sit() is modified to update the value of cumulativeWeight and increment numberOfPersons.

- Class function `averageWeight()` is implemented.

The functions that are changed or added are shown below:

```cpp
// file: newchair.cpp
// chair class definition
#include <cstdlib>
#include <iostream>
#include "newchair.h"

// initialize class variables outside the class
double Chair::cumulativeWeight = 0.0;
long Chair::numberOfPersons = 0;
long Chair::chairCounter = 0;

Chair :: Chair(colors aColor, styles aStyle)
        : acolor(aColor),       // set color to aColor
          astyle(aStyle),       // set style to aStyle
          broken(false),        // set broken to false
          currentLoad(0.0),     // set currentLoad to 0.0
          maxWeight(100.0),     // set weight capacity to 100.0
          personWeight(-1.0),   // set person weight to -1.0
          addedWeight(0.0)      // set added weight to 0.0
{
    ++chairCounter;    // increment count of chairs
    std::cout << "Constructing a Chair object" << std::endl;
}


Chair::~Chair()
{
    --chairCounter;    // decrement count of chairs
    std::cout << "Destroying Chair object"
              << "Active Chair objects: " << chairCounter
              << std::endl;
}

double Chair::sit(double weightOfPerson)
{
    if(broken)
    {
        std::cout << "Cannot sit on a broken chair!" << std::endl;
        return currentLoad;
    }
```

```
   if(!(personWeight < 0.0))
   {
      std::cout << "This chair is taken!" << std::endl;
      return currentLoad;
   }

   personWeight = weightOfPerson;  // save value of person weight
   cumulativeWeight += weightOfPerson;
   ++numberOfPersons;

   return setCurrentWeight();
}

long Chair::activeChairs()
{
   return chairCounter;
}

double Chair::averageWeight()
{
   if( numberOfPersons == 0 )
     return 0;
   else
     return cumulativeWeight / numberOfPersons;
}
```

The main program is changed to print number of active chairs and the average weight of users:

```
#include <iostream>
#include "newchair.h"

int main()
{
   Chair aChair(Chair::colors::red, Chair::styles::modern);
   aChair.sit(50.0);       // person of weight 50 sits on chair
   aChair.addWeight(25.0); // add 25 additional weight
   std::cout << std::endl << "Properties of aChair:"
             << std::endl
             << "Weight : " << aChair.currentWeight()
             << std::endl
             << "Color : " << (int)aChair.color() << std::endl
             << "Style : " << (int)aChair.style()
             << std::endl << std::endl;
```

```
    Chair chair2;        // use default constructor
    chair2.sit(150.0);  // the chair will break. Capacity = 100.0
    chair2.refurbish(); // make the chair new again

    chair2.setColor(Chair::colors::green)
          .setStyle(Chair::styles::modern)
          .clear();
    std::cout << std::endl << "Properties of Chair2:"
              << std::endl
              << "Weight : " << chair2.currentWeight()
              << std::endl
              << "Color : " << (int)chair2.color() << std::endl
              << "Style : " << (int)chair2.style()
              << std::endl  << std::endl;

    std::cout << std::endl
              << "Active Chairs : " << Chair::chairsActive()
              << std::endl
              << "Average Weight: " << Chair::averageWeight()
              << std::endl << std::endl;

    return EXIT_SUCCESS;
}
```

The changes are highlighted in bold.

We changed the definition and implementation of the Chair class to add new capability to the class but the code from the previous main program still worked. This was possible because we only added new functions to the class interface without changing the old class interface in any way. The changes were local to the class and did not affect the code using the class. This localization makes C++ programs easy to modify and maintain.

5.7   Hiding Implementation Details

We do not want to expose the details of our implementation of the Chair class to the users of our class. However, the header file chair.h which is available to the users divulges the details of our design decisions. How do we hide these details? One way is to use two classes to separate the class interface from the detailed implementation:

1. We define a new class named `Chair_Impl` which contains the full implementation of the `Chair` class. The `Chair_Impl` class does everything that the original `Chair` class did. Therefore, the contents of `chair_impl.h` are the same as the original `chair.h` and the implementation code in `chair_impl.cpp` is the same as in the original `chair.cpp`.

2. The `Chair` class definition is changed to contain only the public class interface methods and a private state variable pointing to an object of `Chair_Impl` class. We will have to implement a copy constructor for the modified `Chair` class because it now contains a pointer member.

3. A forward declaration for the `Chair_Impl` class is used in header file `chair.h`. We do not have to include the full header file `Chair_Impl.h` because we only use a pointer to `Chair_Impl` in `Chair`. Therefore, implementation details are not exposed to the user.

4. The `Chair` class interface methods *delegate* the actual work to the methods of the `Chair_Impl` class by calling the corresponding methods in the `Chair_Impl` class in a manner similar to delegating constructors we discussed earlier. This procedure is called *function forwarding*. Therefore, the code in `chair.cpp` does not depend on or expose implementation details.

5.7.1   Chair Class definition

The modified `Chair` class definition is as follows:

```
// file: chair.h
// Chair class definition
#ifndef CHAIR_DEL_H
#define CHAIR_DEL_H

class Chair_Impl;  // forward declaration of implementation class
#include "ChairProperties.h"

class Chair
{
private:
   std::unique_ptr<Chair_Impl> chairImpl; // smart pointer to
                                          // implementation class

public:
```

```
    // constructors and destructor
    Chair();
    Chair(ChairProperties::colors aColor,
          ChairProperties::styles aStyle);
      Chair(Chair& aChair);        // copy constructor
    ~Chair();

    // methods
    double  sit(double weightOfPerson);
    double  getOff();
    double  addWeight(double aWeight);
    double  removeWeight(double aWeight);
    double  currentWeight() const;
    bool    isBroken() const;
    bool    isSitting() const; // true if person seated
    void    clear();                 // remove all load from chair
    void    refurbish();             // make the chair new again!

    // accessor methods for private state variables
    ChairProperties::colors color() const;
    Chair& setColor(ChairProperties::colors aColor);
    ChairProperties::styles style() const;
    Chair& setStyle(ChairProperties::styles aStyle);
    double capacity() const;
    Chair& setCapacity(double limit);
};
#endif
```

The header file chair.h does not reveal any implementation details.

5.7.2   Chair_Impl Class Definition

The Chair_Impl class is defined as follows:

```
// file: chair_impl.h
// Chair_Impl class definition
#ifndef CHAIR_IMPL_H
#define CHAIR_IMPL_H

#include "ChairProperties.h"

class Chair_Impl
{
```

```
private:        // all state variables are made private
    ChairProperties::colors acolor;
    ChairProperties::styles astyle;
    bool            broken;
    double          currentLoad;
    double          maxWeight;
    double          personWeight;
    double          addedWeight;

protected:
    double          setCurrentWeight();

public:
    // constructors and destructor
    Chair_Impl();
    Chair_Impl(ChairProperties::colors aColor,
      ChairProperties::styles aStyle);
    ~Chair_Impl();                      // destructor

    // methods
    double  sit(double weightOfPerson);
    double  getOff();
    double  addWeight(double aWeight);
    double  removeWeight(double aWeight);
    double  currentWeight() const;
    bool    isBroken() const;
    bool    isSitting() const; // true if person seated
    void clear();                   // remove all load from chair
    void refurbish();               // make the chair new again!

    // accessor methods for private data members
    ChairProperties::colors color() const;
    Chair_Impl& setColor(ChairProperties::colors aColor);
    ChairProperties::styles style() const;
    Chair_Impl& setStyle(ChairProperties::styles aStyle);
    double capacity() const;
    Chair_Impl& setCapacity(double limit);
};
#endif
```

The `chair_impl.h` header file contains all implementation details.

5.7.3 ChairProperties Enumerations

The enum definitions for `colors` and `styles` are moved to a separate file and enclosed in a `ChairProperties` class:

```
// file: chairproperties.h
// Chair_Impl class definition
#ifndef CHAIR_PROP_H
#define CHAIR_PROP_H

class ChairProperties
{
public:
    enum class styles { basic, modern, traditional };
    enum class colors { black, white, red, green, blue };
};
#endif
```

5.7.4 Chair Class Implementation

The implementation of the modified `Chair` class using function forwarding is given below. This header file `chair_impl.h` is required for the implementation of the `Chair` class and is included in `chair.cpp`.

```
// file: chair.cpp
// Chair class implementation

#include "stdafx.h"
#include "chair_impl.h"  // chair implementation class
#include "chair.h"
#include <cstdlib>
#include <iostream>

Chair::Chair()
    : Chair(ChairProperties::colors::black,
        ChairProperties::styles::basic)
{
}

Chair::Chair(ChairProperties::colors aColor,
            ChairProperties::styles aStyle)
{
    // Initialize pointer to chair implementation class
```

```cpp
    chairImpl = std::unique_ptr<Chair_Impl>(
                        new Chair_Impl(aColor, aStyle));
}

// copy constructor creates a copy of a chair
// creates new chair with same capacity, color and style
Chair::Chair(Chair& aChair)
{
    chairImpl = std::unique_ptr<Chair_Impl>(new Chair_Impl());
    chairImpl->setCapacity(aChair.capacity());
    chairImpl->setColor(aChair.color());
    chairImpl->setStyle(aChair.style());
}

Chair::~Chair()
{
}

double Chair::sit(double weightOfPerson)
{
    return chairImpl->sit(weightOfPerson);
}

double Chair::addWeight(double aWeight)
{
    return chairImpl->addWeight(aWeight);
}

double Chair::getOff()
{
    return chairImpl->getOff();
}

double Chair::removeWeight(double aWeight)
{
    return chairImpl->removeWeight(aWeight);
}

double Chair::currentWeight() const
{
    return chairImpl->currentWeight();
}

bool Chair::isBroken() const
{
```

```cpp
    return chairImpl->isBroken();
}

bool Chair::isSitting() const
{
    return chairImpl->isSitting();
}

void Chair::clear()
{
    chairImpl->clear();
}

void Chair::refurbish()
{
    chairImpl->refurbish();
}

ChairProperties::colors Chair::color() const
{
    return        chairImpl->color();
}

Chair& Chair::setColor(ChairProperties::colors aColor)
{
    chairImpl->setColor(aColor);
    return *this;
}

ChairProperties::styles Chair::style() const
{
    return chairImpl->style();
}

Chair& Chair::setStyle(ChairProperties::styles aStyle)
{
    chairImpl->setStyle(aStyle);
    return *this;
}

double Chair::capacity() const
{
    return chairImpl->capacity();
}
```

```
Chair& Chair::setCapacity(double limit)
{
    chairImpl->setCapacity(limit);
    return *this;
}
```

The class user does not have access to the **chair.cpp** file so implementation details in the included **chair_impl.h** header file are not exposed. The code itself is also not dependent on any implementation details.

5.7.5   Chair_Impl Class Implementation

All implementation details are in the **Chair_Impl** class which the user does not have access to. The code is the same as for the original **Chair** class as shown below:

```
// file: chair_impl.cpp
// Chair_Impl class implementation

#include "stdafx.h"
#include "chair_impl.h"
#include <cstdlib>
#include <iostream>

Chair_Impl::Chair_Impl()
    : Chair_Impl(ChairProperties::colors::black,
ChairProperties::styles::basic)
{
}

Chair_Impl::Chair_Impl(ChairProperties::colors aColor,
ChairProperties::styles aStyle)
    : acolor(aColor),       // set color to aColor
    astyle(aStyle),         // set style to aStyle
    broken(false),          // set broken to false
    currentLoad(0.0),       // set currentLoad to 0.0
    maxWeight(100.0),       // set weight capacity to 100.0
    personWeight(-1.0),     // set person weight to -1.0
    addedWeight(0.0)        // set added weight to 0.0
{
}

Chair_Impl::~Chair_Impl()
{
```

```
}

double Chair_Impl::sit(double weightOfPerson)
{
    if (broken)
    {
        std::cout << "Cannot sit on a broken chair!" <<
std::endl;
        return currentLoad;
    }

    if (!(personWeight < 0.0))
    {
        std::cout << "This chair is taken!" << std::endl;
        return currentLoad;
    }

    personWeight = weightOfPerson;
    return setCurrentWeight();
}

double Chair_Impl::addWeight(double aWeight)
{
    if (broken)
    {
        std::cout << "Cannot add weight to a broken chair!" <<
std::endl;
        return currentLoad;
    }

    addedWeight += aWeight;
    return setCurrentWeight();
}

double Chair_Impl::getOff()
{
    if (broken)
    {
        std::cout << "The chair is broken!" << std::endl;
        return currentLoad;
    }

    if (personWeight < 0.0)
    {
```

```cpp
            std::cout << "No one is sitting on the chair!" <<
std::endl;
            return currentLoad;
    }

    personWeight = -1.0;
    return setCurrentWeight();
}

double Chair_Impl::removeWeight(double aWeight)
{
    if (broken)
    {
            std::cout << "The chair is broken!" << std::endl;
            return currentLoad;
    }

    addedWeight -= aWeight;
    if (addedWeight < 0.0)
    {
            addedWeight = 0.0;
    }

    return setCurrentWeight();
}

double Chair_Impl::currentWeight() const
{
    return currentLoad;
}

double Chair_Impl::setCurrentWeight()
{
    if (personWeight < 0.0)
    {
            currentLoad = addedWeight;
    }
    else
    {
            currentLoad = personWeight + addedWeight;
    }

    if (currentLoad > maxWeight)
    {
            broken = true;
```

```
            std::cout << std::endl
                << "Weight " << currentLoad << " > "
                << "Capacity " << maxWeight
                << ". The chair broke!"
                << std::endl;
    }
    return currentLoad;
}

bool Chair_Impl::isBroken() const
{
    return broken;
}

bool Chair_Impl::isSitting() const
{
    if (personWeight < 0.0)
            return false;
    else
            return true;
}

void Chair_Impl::clear()
{
    currentLoad = 0.0;
}

void Chair_Impl::refurbish()
{
    acolor = ChairProperties::colors::black;
    astyle = ChairProperties::styles::basic;
    broken = false;          // set broken to false
    currentLoad = 0.0;       // set currentLoad to 0.0
    maxWeight = 100.0;       // set weight capacity to 100.0
    personWeight = -1.0;     // set weight of last sit to -1.0
    addedWeight = 0.0;       // set weight of last sit to 0.0
}

ChairProperties::colors Chair_Impl::color() const
{
    return acolor;
}

Chair_Impl& Chair_Impl::setColor(ChairProperties::colors aColor)
{
```

```
    acolor = aColor;
    return *this;
}


ChairProperties::styles Chair_Impl::style() const
{
    return astyle;
}


Chair_Impl& Chair_Impl::setStyle(ChairProperties::styles aStyle)
{
    astyle = aStyle;
    return *this;
}


double Chair_Impl::capacity() const
{
    return maxWeight;
}


Chair_Impl& Chair_Impl::setCapacity(double limit)
{
    maxWeight = limit;
    return *this;
}
```

5.7.6   Using the new Chair Class

The main program using the new Chair class stays the same except for the use of ChairProperties class to access styles and colors:

```
// Ch06_ChairFunctionForwarding.cpp

#include "stdafx.h"
#include "chair.h"
#include <iostream>

int main()
{
    Chair aChair(ChairProperties::colors::red,
                 ChairProperties::styles::traditional);
    aChair.sit(50.0);       // person of weight 50 sits on chair
    aChair.addWeight(25.0); // add 25 additional weight
```

```
    std::cout << std::endl << "Properties of aChair:"
        << std::endl
        << "Weight : " << aChair.currentWeight()
        << std::endl
        << "Color : " << (int)aChair.color() << std::endl
        << "Style : " << (int)aChair.style()
        << std::endl << std::endl;

    Chair chair2;        // use default constructor
    chair2.sit(150.0);   // the chair will break. Capacity = 100.0
    chair2.refurbish();  // make the chair new again

    // chaining of function calls sequence breaks
    // at clear() because it returns void and not Chair&
    chair2.setColor(ChairProperties::colors::green)
        .setStyle(ChairProperties::styles::modern)
        .clear();
    std::cout << std::endl << "Properties of Chair2:"
        << std::endl
        << "Weight : " << chair2.currentWeight()
        << std::endl
        << "Color : " << (int)chair2.color() << std::endl
        << "Style : " << (int)chair2.style()
        << std::endl << std::endl;

    return EXIT_SUCCESS;
}
```

The changes are highlighted in bold.

5.8   Summary

Some recommended class design practices are as follows:

1. Always define a default constructor for your class. If you do not want the users of your class to create arrays of objects of your class, declare the default constructor to be private.

2. If your class uses pointers as state variables, always define a copy constructor for your class. If you do not want the users of your class to initialize objects during declaration or pass objects by value as function arguments, declare the copy constructor to be private.

3. If your class uses pointers as state variables, always define an assignment operator for your class. If you do not want the users of your class to copy objects by assignment, declare the assignment operator to be private.

4. Use forward declarations and function forwarding to separate definition of the class interface from its implementation. This hides implementation details from users of the class.

6   Reusing Code

6.1   Introduction

In the previous chapter, we modified the original `Chair` class to add more capability. However, if we want to use objects of both the original `Chair` class and the better chair class in our programs, we will have to keep the old `Chair` class and create a new class containing the modified code. We will end up with two independent classes that have a lot of common code. Any changes to the common code will have to be made to code in both the classes. The copies of common code will grow as we add new types of chairs. This proliferation of copies of common code creates a code management nightmare and increases the probability of errors during code modifications. We need a mechanism which allows us to reuse common code in all `Chair` based classed.

Object oriented programming provides two mechanisms for reusing existing code: inheritance and composition. We will look at both in this chapter.

6.2   Inheritance

New classes can be defined in terms of existing classes through the mechanism of *inheritance*. Inheritance is implemented in C++ by *class derivation*. An existing class, called the *base class* (also called the *parent class* or *superclass*), is used as the starting point and a new class called the *derived class* (also called the *child class* or *subclass*) is derived through inheritance. The derived class has an *"is a"* or *"can be used as"* relationship to the base class. For example, a simple chair is a `Chair` and the better chair also is a `Chair` and can be used as a simple `Chair` if its added capabilities (counting and average user weight tracking) are ignored. Therefore, we can use inheritance to implement the better chair as a derived class using `Chair` as the base class.

The derived classes extend the definition of the base class in three ways:

- Add new state variables
- Add new methods

- Override existing methods in the base class by writing new methods that hide the base class methods

New code is required only for the new additions. The code for the base class gets used as is.

Inheritance can be used to implement hierarchies of classes for different applications, with the classes at the bottom of the hierarchy inheriting capabilities from the classes above.

6.2.1   Specifying Inheritance

The inheritance relationship is specified in a *derivation list* provided in the class definition of the derived class. The derivation list starts after a colon (:) following the name of the derived class. For example, a `SmartChair` class may be derived from the `Chair` class as follows:

```cpp
class SmartChair : public Chair
{
 // new state or class variables

 // new methods

 // overridden methods

}
```

The keyword `public` specifies the type of inheritance and controls the visibility of `public` and `protected` members of the base class in the derived class. The derived class inherits the public interface of the base class and it becomes a part of the public interface of the derived class. When we create an object of a derived class, it contains sub-objects of the all the base classes.

6.2.2   Types of Inheritance

C++ has three types of inheritance:

1. **Public:** All public members of the base classes are visible as public members of the derived class. All protected members of the base classes are visible as protected members of the derived class. Public

inheritance establishes an *"is a"* relationship between the derived class and the base class.

2. **Private**: All public and protected members of the base classes are visible as private members of the derived class. Private inheritance does not establish an *"is a"* relationship between the derived class and the base class.

3. **Protected**: All public and protected members of the base classes are visible as protected members of the derived class. Protected inheritance does not establish an *"is a"* relationship between the derived class and the base class.

The private members of a base classes are never visible in a derived class.

6.2.3   Multiple Inheritance

In C++, a class can inherit from several base classes, with the names of all the base classes specified in a comma separated derivation list. This is called *multiple inheritance*. A major problem with multiple inheritance is as follows:

```
class A : public B {}     // class A inherits from B
class C : public B {}     // class C inherits from B
class D : public A, C {} // class D inherits from A and C
```

Class D ends up using class B as a base class twice, through classes A and C. When we create an instance of class D, we will end up with two sub-objects of class B. Which one to use? To avoid this problem, we can declare class B to be a virtual base class of classes A and C as shown below:

```
class A : public virtual B  // class A inherits from B
class C : public virtual B  // class C inherits from B
class D : public A, C        // class D inherits from A and C
```

In this case, only one sub-object of class B will be created when we create an instance of D. Virtual base classes combined with private inheritance are very useful for hiding implementation details. We will look at it in more detail in Chapter 7.

6.2.4   Overriding Base Class Members

We can declare a state variable or a method in the derived class that is an exact duplicate of a visible member of the base class. This is called *overriding* a base class member. The derived class member *hides* the base class member. All references to the overridden member will use the derived class member. The hidden member can still be accessed through the scope resolution operator :: using a syntax of the form `BaseClass::hiddenMember`, where `BaseClass` is the name of the base class.

6.2.5   Derived Class Constructors

When we create instances of the derived class by declaring a variable of the derived class or by using the `new` operator, the compiler first calls a constructor of the base class to create a base class sub-object and then the constructor of the derived class to create the instance of the derived class. This sequence of operations is required because a derived class is built upon the base class. We can also explicitly invoke a base class constructor from a constructor of the derived class. If this explicit call is not made, the compiler will call the default constructor of the base class to create the base class sub-object.

6.2.6   Derived Class Destructors

When an object of a derived class is destroyed because it goes out of scope or when the `delete` operator is used, the C++ compiler does the following:
1. The destructor of the derived class is called to destroy the object of the derived class.
2. The destructor of the base class is called to destroy the base class sub-object.

6.2.7   Example: A SmartChair Class

We will define a `SmartChair` class that keeps count of the number of active chairs and the average weight of the users of our chairs. `SmartChair` is defined as a derived class based on the `Chair` class:

```
// file: smartchair.h
```

```
// SmartChair class definition
#ifndef SMARTCHAIR_H
#define SMARTCHAIR_H

#include "chair.h"        // required for Chair class

class SmartChair : public Chair
{
 private:
   static double cumulativeWeight;   // class variable
   static long numberOfPersons;      // class variable
   static long chairCounter;         // class variable

 public:
   SmartChair();
   SmartChair(colors aColor, styles aStyle);
   ~CountedChair();

   double sit(double personWeight); // overridden method

   static long activeChairs();       // class method
   static double averageWeight();    // class method
 };
#endif
```

The SmartChair class has two constructors similar to those in the Chair class and extends the Chair class as follows:

- Adds class variable cumulativeWeight.

- Adds class variable numberOfPersons.

- Adds class variable chairCounter.

- Adds class method activeChairs().

- Adds class method averageWeight().

- Overrides the sit()method provided by the base Chair class.

The SmartChair class is implemented as follows:

```
// file: smartchair.cpp
// chair class definition
#include <cstdlib>
#include <iostream>
#include "smartchair.h"

// initialize class variables outside the class
```

```cpp
double SmartChair::cumulativeWeight = 0.0;
long    SmartChair::numberOfPersons = 0;
long    SmartChair::chairCounter = 0;

SmartChair::SmartChair()
             : SmartChair(colors::black, styles::basic)
{
   std::cout << "Default Constructor: SmartChair" << std::endl;
}

SmartChair::SmartChair(colors aColor, styles aStyle)
             : Chair(aColor, aStyle)
{
   ++chairCounter;    // increment count of chairs
   std::cout << "Constructing a SmartChair object" << std::endl;
}

SmartChair::~SmartChair()
{
   --chairCounter;    // decrement count of chairs
   std::cout << "Destroying Chair object"
             << "Active Chair objects: " << chairCounter
             << std::endl;
}

double SmartChair::sit(double weightOfPerson)
{
   std::cout << std::endl
             << "In sit() function in SmartChair"
             << std::endl;
   cumulativeWeight += weightOfPerson;
   ++numberOfPersons;

   return Chair::sit(weightOfPerson);
}

long SmartChair::chairsActive()
{
   return chairCounter;
}

double SmartChair::averageWeight()
{
   if( numberOfPersons == 0 )
     return 0;
```

```
    else
      return cumulativeWeight / numberOfPersons;
}
```

The overridden `sit()` method does the following:

1. Prints a message to show it has been called.

2. Updates the cumulative weight of users sitting on the chair.

3. Increments the user count.

4. Calls the base class method `Chair::sit()` to set the weight of the person sitting on the chair.

Overridden methods in derived classes frequently call their base class counterparts to use the functionality of the base class in addition to new features added in the derived class.

The `main` program stays the same as in the better Chair example in Chapter 5 except that we create `SmartChair` objects instead of `Chair` objects:

```cpp
#include <cstdlib>
#include <iostream>
#include "smartchair.h"

// the main function
int main()
{
    SmartChair aChair(Chair::colors::red, Chair::styles::modern);
    aChair.sit(50.0);       // person of weight 50 sits on chair
    aChair.addWeight(25.0); // add 25 additional weight
    std::cout << std::endl << "Properties of aChair:"
              << std::endl
              << "Weight : " << aChair.currentWeight()
              << std::endl
              << "Color : " << (int)aChair.color() << std::endl
              << "Style : " << (int)aChair.style()
              << std::endl << std::endl;

    SmartChair chair2;   // use default constructor
    chair2.sit(150.0);   // the chair will break. Capacity = 100.0
    chair2.refurbish();  // make the chair new again

    chair2.setColor(Chair::colors::green)
          .setStyle(Chair::styles::modern);
          .clear();      // set weight to 0.0
    std::cout << std::endl << "Properties of Chair2:"
```

```
                    << std::endl
                    << "Weight : " << chair2.currentWeight()
                    << std::endl
                    << "Color : " << (int)chair2.color() << std::endl
                    << "Style : " << (int)chair2.style()
                    << std::endl  << std::endl;

    std::cout << std::endl
                    << "Active Chairs : " << SmartChair::chairsActive()
                    << std::endl
                    << "Average Weight: " << SmartChair::averageWeight()
                    << std::endl << std::endl;

    return EXIT_SUCCESS;
}
```

The changes are highlighted in bold. The output is exactly the same as the better Chair example in Chapter 5.

6.2.8   Object Slicing

As stated before, a derived class object has an *"is a"* or a *"can be used as"* relationship with the base class. Therefore, a derived class object can be assigned to a variable of the base class without requiring an explicit cast as shown in the code below:

```
Chair aChair;
SmartChair aSmartChair;

aChair = aSmartChair;   // OK. A SmartChair "is a" Chair
```

The aChair object can now be used to access the public interface of aSmartChair. Only those members which were inherited from Chair will be accessible through aChair. This is called *object slicing*: the aSmartChair object is sliced by the aChair variable, leaving behind only the public interface of the Chair class. This property of class derivation is used to write generic code as shown in the function below:

```
void breakAnyChair(Chair& aChair) // need a pointer or reference
{
    aChair.addWeight(10000.0);      // enough weight to break chair!
}
```

The "*can be used as*" relationship can be implemented only through a pointer or reference to an object of the base class. Therefore, the parameter to the function breakAnyChair() cannot be an object of class Chair. The function uses the public interface of the Chair class to accomplish its purpose. Therefore, it will work with objects of the Chair class and objects of classes that use Chair as a public base class. Function calls breakChair(aChair) and breakChair(aSmartChair) both work properly.

6.3   Composition

We can also create new classes and reuse code by *composition*. This represents a "*is a part of*" or "*is used by*" relationship between classes. New classes are created by combining existing classes. For example, a class representing a car may be created as follows:

```
// forward declarations
Class Body;
Class Engine;
Class Tire;
Class Seats;
...

class Car
{
 private:
   string make;
   string model;
   ...

 public:
   Body& aBody;
   Engine& anEngine;
   Tire& tires;
   Seats& frontSeat;
   Seats& backseat;
   ...
};
```

Here we have a set of predefined classes (Body, Tire, Seats, Engine, etc.) that are used to compose a Car. The Car class uses the existing code for component classes without modification and adds new code specific to a car as a whole such as the **make** and **model**. The component classes are *a part of* (or *are used by*) the enclosing **Car** class. When we create an instance of a class defined using composition, the compiler creates a member sub-object for all the member classes.

6.3.1 Example: A ReclingingChair Class

We will create a **ReclingingChair** class by composition. The **Chair**, **Chair_Impl** and **ChairProperties** classes we defined in Chapter 5 to demonstrate function forwarding are used as the starting point. **Chair_Impl** and **ChairProperties** classes are reused without any changes. The **Chair** class is modified to create the **ReclingingChair** class.

We first define a simple **Recliner** class that represents the reclining mechanism used by the chair. The class sets and returns the value, in degrees, of the recline angle of the seatback:

```
// File: recliner.h - Recliner class definition
//
#ifndef RECLINER_H
#define RECLINER_H

class Recliner
{
private:
    int seatbackAngle;

public:
    Recliner();
    Recliner(int anAngle);
    ~Recliner();
    void setAngle(int anAngle);
    int angle();
    void reset();
};
#endif
```

The **ReclingingChair** class is defined as follows:

```
// file: recliningchair.h
// ReclingingChair class definition
#ifndef RECLINING_CHAIR_H
#define RECLINING_CHAIR_H
```

```
class Recliner;     // forward declaration for Recliner class
class Chair_Impl;   // forward declaration for Chair_Impl class

#include "ChairProperties.h"
#include <memory>

class RecliningChair
{
private:
    // data members pointing to component objects
    std::unique_ptr<Chair_Impl> chairImpl;
    std::unique_ptr<Recliner> aRecliner;

public:
    // constructors and destructor
    RecliningChair();
    RecliningChair(ChairProperties::colors aColor,
                   ChairProperties::styles aStyle);
    RecliningChair(RecliningChair &aChair); // copy constructor
    ~RecliningChair();                      // destructor

    // chair methods
    double  sit(double weightOfPerson);
    double  getOff();
    double  addWeight(double aWeight);
    double  removeWeight(double aWeight);
    double  currentWeight() const;
    bool    isBroken() const;
    bool    isSitting() const;      // true if person seated
    void    clear();                // remove all load from chair
    void    refurbish();            // make the chair new again!

    // accessor functions for private data members
    ChairProperties::colors color() const;
    RecliningChair& setColor(ChairProperties::colors aColor);
    ChairProperties::styles style() const;
    RecliningChair& setStyle(ChairProperties::styles aStyle);
    double capacity() const;
    RecliningChair& setCapacity(double limit);

    // reclining methods
    void    setRecline(int anAngle);  // recline the seatback
    int     recline();                // get recline angle
};
#endif// file: recliningchair.h
```

The changes made to the Chair class are highlighted in bold. We have added a Recliner object as a member of the class to provide the reclining capability for chairs. Two new public class interface methods setRecline() and recline() provide the class interface for chair users to set and query the reclining angle. The remaining class interface is the same as the Chair class.

The Recliner class is implemented as follows:

```
// File: recliner.cpp
// Recliner class implementation

#include "stdafx.h"
#include "recliner.h"

Recliner::Recliner()
        : Recliner(0)
{}

Recliner::Recliner(int anAngle)
{
    seatbackAngle = anAngle;
}

Recliner::~Recliner()
{}

void Recliner::setAngle(int anAngle)
{
    seatbackAngle = anAngle;
}

int Recliner::angle()
{
    return seatbackAngle;
}

void Recliner::reset()
{
    seatbackAngle = 0;
}
```

The implementation of the RecliningChair class is as follows:

```
// file: RecliningChair.cpp
// RecliningChair class implementation
```

```
#include "stdafx.h"
#include "recliningchair.h"
#include "recliner.h"
#include "chair_impl.h"
#include <cstdlib>
#include <iostream>

RecliningChair::RecliningChair()
    : RecliningChair(ChairProperties::colors::black,
                        ChairProperties::styles::basic)
{
}

RecliningChair::RecliningChair(ChairProperties::colors aColor,
                                ChairProperties::styles aStyle)
{
    // create Chair_Impl and Recliner objects
    chairImpl = std::unique_ptr<Chair_Impl>(
                                new Chair_Impl(aColor, aStyle));
    aRecliner = std::unique_ptr<Recliner>(new Recliner());
}

RecliningChair::RecliningChair(RecliningChair& aChair)
{
    chairImpl = std::unique_ptr<Chair_Impl>(new Chair_Impl());
    chairImpl->setCapacity(aChair.capacity());
    chairImpl->setColor(aChair.color());
    chairImpl->setStyle(aChair.style());

    // copy recline angle
    aRecliner = std::unique_ptr<Recliner>(new Recliner());
    aRecliner->setAngle(aChair.recline());
}

RecliningChair::~RecliningChair()
{
}

int RecliningChair::recline()
{
    return aRecliner->angle();
}

void RecliningChair::setRecline(int anAngle)
```

```
{
    return aRecliner->setAngle(anAngle);
}


double RecliningChair::sit(double weightOfPerson)
{
    return chairImpl->sit(weightOfPerson);
}

double RecliningChair::addWeight(double aWeight)
{
    return chairImpl->addWeight(aWeight);
}

double RecliningChair::getOff()
{
    return chairImpl->getOff();
}

double RecliningChair::removeWeight(double aWeight)
{
    return chairImpl->removeWeight(aWeight);
}

double RecliningChair::currentWeight() const
{
    return chairImpl->currentWeight();
}

bool RecliningChair::isBroken() const
{
    return chairImpl->isBroken();
}

bool RecliningChair::isSitting() const
{
    return chairImpl->isSitting();
}

void RecliningChair::clear()
{
    chairImpl->clear();
}
```

```
void RecliningChair::refurbish()
{
    aRecliner->reset();
    chairImpl->refurbish();
}

ChairProperties::colors RecliningChair::color() const
{
    return       chairImpl->color();
}

RecliningChair& RecliningChair::setColor(ChairProperties::colors
aColor)
{
    chairImpl->setColor(aColor);
    return *this;
}

ChairProperties::styles RecliningChair::style() const
{
    return chairImpl->style();
}

RecliningChair& RecliningChair::setStyle(ChairProperties::styles
aStyle)
{
    chairImpl->setStyle(aStyle);
    return *this;
}

double RecliningChair::capacity() const
{
    return chairImpl->capacity();
}

RecliningChair& RecliningChair::setCapacity(double limit)
{
    chairImpl->setCapacity(limit);
    return *this;
}
```

The changes to the code for the Chair class are highlighted in bold.

The main function is also remains the same as in Chapter 5, except for additional statements to use the reclining capability:

```cpp
// Ch06_RecliningChair.cpp
//
#include "stdafx.h"
#include "recliningchair.h"
#include <cstdlib>
#include <iostream>

int main()
{
    RecliningChair aChair(ChairProperties::colors::red,
                          ChairProperties::styles::traditional);
    aChair.sit(50.0);       // person of weight 50 sits on chair
    aChair.addWeight(25.0); // add 25 additional weight
    aChair.setRecline(20);  // recline seatbak 20 deg
    std::cout << std::endl << "Properties of aChair:"
          << std::endl
          << "Weight : " << aChair.currentWeight()
          << std::endl
          << "Color : " << (int)aChair.color() << std::endl
          << "Style : " << (int)aChair.style()
          << std::endl
          << "Recline : " << aChair.recline()
          << std::endl << std::endl;

    RecliningChair chair2; // use default constructor
    chair2.sit(150.0);  // the chair will break. Capacity = 100.0
    chair2.refurbish(); // make the chair new again

    // chaining of function calls sequence breaks
    // at clear() because it returns void and not Chair&
    chair2.setColor(ChairProperties::colors::green)
          .setStyle(ChairProperties::styles::modern)
          .clear();
    std::cout << std::endl << "Properties of Chair2:"
          << std::endl
          << "Weight : " << chair2.currentWeight()
          << std::endl
          << "Color : " << (int)chair2.color() << std::endl
          << "Style : " << (int)chair2.style()
          << std::endl
          << "Recline : " << chair2.recline()
          << std::endl << std::endl;

    return EXIT_SUCCESS;
}
```

The changes are highlighted in bold.

As we can see, composition is just as effective as inheritance in adding new capabilities and reusing code.

6.4   Composition or Inheritance?

Most real world objects contain simpler component objects. Composition is pervasive. The hierarchical classifications that we model using inheritance usually involve relatively complex objects. Our programs will probably use both composition and inheritance.

We should keep the following points in mind:

- Composition allows us to use small, independent, single-responsibility classes to create our models. This decouples the different capabilities of our model, making it easy to manage and evolve the model. However, as the number of components classes grow, modeling the interactions between them may become more complex and difficult to program.

- Inheritance is a powerful tool when we want to model an "*is a*" relationship. However, the classes higher up in a class hierarchy impose restrictions on what the derived classes can do and requirements for what they have to do. This can create problems as the hierarchies grow. The problems can be contained by using shallow hierarchies of classes.

What approach should we take? We should first try to use composition to solve our problem. Inheritance should be introduced if composition alone will not be sufficient or if an "*is a*" relationship is required.

7   Polymorphism

The word polymorphism means one object having many forms. In object oriented programming, it means the ability to use derived class objects through a pointer or a reference to an object of a class higher up in the class hierarchy without losing the class identity of the derived object. In other words, no object slicing. Polymorphism expresses a *"can be used as"* relationship between classes.

7.1   What is Polymorphism

Suppose we have a class `Flowers` that expresses the essence of what makes an object a flower. This class may be used as a public base class for different types of flowers we want to represent. We define the `Flowers` base class as follows:

```
class Flowers
{
 public:
    enum class smells { Tulips, Rose, Jasmine, default };

 private:
    std::string flowerName;

 public:
    Flowers();
    Flowers(const std::string& aName);
    ~Flowers();
    smells smell();
    const std::string& name() const;
    void setName(const std::string& aName);
};
```

The purpose of method `Flowers::smell()` is to return the smell a flower. The implementation of the method will, therefore, be different for each type of derived flower. A Rose cannot smell like a Jasmine! Classes named `Rose` and `Jasmine` using `Flowers` as a public base class may be defined as shown below:

```
class Rose : public Flowers
{
 public:
    Rose();
    Rose(const std::string& aName);
```

```
    ~Rose();
    smells smell();
};

class Jasmine : public Flowers
{
 public:
    Jasmine();
    Jasmine(const std::string& aName);
    ~Jasmine();
    smells smell();
};
```

Both classes override the `Flowers::smell()` method to provide a smell specific to their type. We now write a function that takes a `vector` of pointers to `Flowers` as a parameter and calls the `smell()` method of each flower in the `vector`:

```
void smellFlowers( vector<Flowers*> &flowers )
{
 for(int i =0 ; i < flowers.size(); ++i)
    {
      std::cout << "Smell of a " << flowers[i]->name()
                << " is " << (int)flowers[i]->smell()
                << std::endl;
    }
}
```

In the calling program, the `vector` is filled with pointers to flowers of different types, all of them derived using `Flowers` as a public base class. However, even though we have overridden the `Flowers::smell()` method in each derived class, the call to the `smell()` method in `smellFlowers()` will always call `Flowers::smell()` because of object slicing. This is not the desired behavior. When we call the `smell()` method inside `smellFlowers()`, we want the smell of the specific type of flower added to the vector i.e. a Rose passed in the `vector` should smell like a Rose and a Jasmine should smell like a Jasmine. The `smell()` method in `smellFlowers()` should behave differently for different flowers by calling the `smell()` method of the actual flower even though the call is made through a base class pointer. This ability to modify behavior based on the actual derived class while operating through a pointer or reference to a base class from the same class hierarchy is called *polymorphism*. C++ implements polymorphism using *virtual functions*. The virtual function mechanism ensures that the function provided by the actual class is invoked even if it is called through a base class pointer or reference.

7.2   Virtual Functions

Virtual functions enable us to use the class interface of a base class to write generic code that works for all derived classes that use that class as a public base class. The base class provides an interface that is common to all the classes in the hierarchy and provides a default implementation that is used if the virtual functions are not overridden in a derived class.

For virtual functions, C++ determines at run time which function to call. A table of pointers to virtual functions is maintained for a class. By default, an entry is made for all the virtual functions provided in the base class. If a virtual function is overridden in a derived class, an entry is made in the table listing the name of the derived class and a pointer to the virtual function provided in the derived class. If a virtual function is not overridden in a derived class, the entry for the derived class will point to the virtual function provided in the base class. When a virtual function is called through a base class pointer, the compiler uses the virtual function table to select the proper function to call based on the actual class of the object. This process of deciding which function to run during program execution is called *dynamic binding* or *late binding*.

The destructor for a class that has even one virtual function should always be declared virtual to ensure that proper cleanup occurs. Conversely, if a class does not have any virtual functions, the destructor should not be declared as virtual.

Virtual functions do impose a performance penalty so they should be avoided in situations where maximum performance is a requirement or in classes which will not be a part of inheritance based hierarchies.

7.2.1   Virtual Flowers

We modify the Flowers class to make the smell() function a virtual function as shown below:

```
#ifndef FLOWERS_H
  #define FLOWERS_H
```

```
#include <string>

class Flowers
{
 public:
   enum class smells {Pleasant, Rose, Jasmine, default };

 private:
   std::string flowerName;

 public:
   Flowers();
   Flowers(std::string& aName);
   virtual ~Flowers();      // a virtual destructor
   virtual smells smell();  // a virtual smell() function
   std::string& name() const;
   void setName(const std::string& aName);
};

#endif
```

If a function declared as virtual in the base class is overridden in a derived class, the function must also be declared as virtual in the derived classes. Our derived classes will change accordingly:

```
class Rose : public Flowers
{
 public:
   Rose();
   Rose(const std::string& aName);
   virtual ~Rose();
   virtual smells smell();
};

class Jasmine : public Flowers
{
 public:
   Jasmine();
   Jasmine(const std::string& aName);
   virtual ~Jasmine();
};
```

Note that Jasmine does not override smell(). The three classes are implemented as follows:

```
#include <cstdlib>
#include <iostream>
#include "flowers.h"

Flowers::Flowers()
        : Flowers("Base class flower")
{
}

Flowers::Flowers(std::string& aName)
{
    setNmae();
}

Flowers::~Flowers()
{
}

Flowers::smells Flowers::smell()
{
    return smells::default;
}

const std::string& Flowers::name() const
{
    return flowerName;
}

void Flowers::setName(const std::string& aName)
{
    if(aName.size() > 0)
      flowerName = aName;
    else
      flowerName = "You can call me ...";
}


Rose::Rose()
    : Rose("A Rose by any other name ...")
{
}

Rose::Rose(const std::string& aName)
    : Flowers(aName)
{
```

```
}

Rose::~Rose()
{
}

Flowers::smells Rose::smell()
{
    return smells::Rose;
}

Jasmine::Jasmine()
        : Jasmine("A Default Jasmine")
{
}

Jasmine::Jasmine(const std::string& aName)
        : Flowers(aName)
{
}

Jasmine::~Jasmine()
{
}
```

The main function that demonstrates how smellFlowers() works is given
below:

```
#include <cstdlib>
#include <iostream>
#include <string>
#include <vector>
#include "flowers.h"
#include "rose.h"
#include "jasmine.h"

void smellFlowers(std::vector<Flowers*> &flowers )
{
 for(int i =0 ; i < flowers.size(); ++i)
    {
      std::cout << "Smell of a " << flowers[i]->name()
                << " is " << (int)flowers[i]->smell()
                << std::endl;
    }
}
```

```
// the main function
int main()
{
    // call smellFlowers() with a vector of Roses
    std::cout << std::endl
              << "Calling smellFlowers with Roses"
              << std::endl;
    std::vector<Flowers*> roses(3);    // a vector of Roses
    roses[0] = new Rose("Red Rose");
    roses[1] = new Rose("White Rose");
    roses[2] = new Rose("Yellow Rose");
    smellFlowers(roses);
    std::cout << std::endl;

    // call smellFlowers() with an array of Jasmines
    std::cout << std::endl
              << "Calling smellFlowers with Jasmines"
              << std::endl;
    std::vector<Flowers*> jasmines(3);    // a vector of Jasmines
    jasmines[0] = new Jasmine("Fresh Jasmine");
    jasmines[1] = new Jasmine("California Jasmine");
    jasmines[2] = new Jasmine("New York Jasmine");
    smellFlowers(jasmines);
    std::cout << std::endl;

    return EXIT_SUCCESS;
}
```

The output generated by the main function is given below:

```
Calling smellFlowers with Roses
Smell of a Red Rose is 1
Smell of a White Rose is 1
Smell of a Yellow Rose is 1


Calling smellFlowers with Jasmines
Smell of a Fresh Jasmine is 3
Smell of a California Jasmine is 3
Smell of a New York Jasmine is 3
```

In our example, passing a vector of Rose objects printed the smell of Roses while the Jasmine array printed the smell of base class Flowers. That is exactly what was expected because Jasmine did not override smell().

It does not make sense to print the smell of the base class when a `Jasmine` object is passed to the `smellAll()`. We want to force the users of our `Flowers` base class to always override the virtual `smell()` function in the derived classes. Also, we do not want allow users to create instances of the `Flowers` base class because it is meaningless to do so. Let us see how we can do that.

7.3   Abstract Base Classes

We can make it mandatory to override a virtual function by declaring it to be a *pure virtual function*. Pure virtual functions do not contain any code and serve as placeholders in a base class for functions that must be overridden in a derived class. If a class has even one pure virtual function in its declaration, it is called an *abstract base class*. We cannot create instances of an abstract class. If a derived class does not override a pure virtual function, that class also becomes an abstract class. We will refer to non-abstract classes as *concrete classes* to distinguish them from abstract classes in situations where this distinction has to be emphasized.

We modify our `Flowers` class again with `smell()` as a pure virtual function:

```
class Flowers
{
 private:
   string aName;

 public:
   Flowers();
   Flowers(string aName, short aSmell);
   virtual ~Flowers();
   virtual short smell() = 0;   // pure virtual function
   string name() const;
   void setName(const string aName);
};
```

In our flowers example above, `Jasmine` did not override `smell()`. Therefore, now that `smell()` is a pure virtual function, `Jasmine` also becomes an abstract class. We can no longer create `Flower` and `Jasmine` objects, only `Rose` objects. So our `main` program will not work until we override `smell()` in `Jasmine`.

7.4 Modelling Common Behavior

We can design abstract base classes that contain only pure virtual functions with the sole purpose of providing a public class interface (a set of public methods) that is shared by and must be implemented by all classes derived from these abstract class. We will refer to these classes as *interface base classes* or simply *Interfaces*. We cannot create instances of an Interface because it is an abstract class.

An Interface has the following properties:

1. All methods of the class are pure virtual functions. In general, these methods should not contain any code. Any code that is included should be defined solely in terms of other methods specified in the interface.

2. The class has no state variables.

3. The class has no constructors.

We can use multiple inheritance to implement multiple interfaces in a derived class using Interfaces as public virtual base classes. The instances of the derived class may be used through pointers or references to any of the Interfaces from which the class is derived.

Interfaces provide us with a powerful mechanism to write generic code that is not dependent of any implementation details. Whenever possible, we should:

- Use Interfaces to define the public interface of a class.

- Use pointers and references to Interfaces instead of concrete classes as data members of a class.

- Use pointers and references to Interfaces instead of concrete classes as formal parameters in functions.

- Use Interfaces instead of concrete classes as return types of functions.

- Write code in the body of a function using Interface members.

7.5 Interfaces and Composition

We will change the `RecliningChair` class from Chapter 6 to use interfaces as follows:

- Define an `IChair` interface to represent the functions of a chair.

- Define an `IRecline` interface to represent the reclining function in a chair.

- Define an `IRecliner` interface to represent the functions of the reclining mechanism.

- Implement the `RecliningChair` using `IChair` and `IRecline`.

- Implement the `Chair_Impl` class using `IChair`.

- Implement the `Recliner` class using `IRecliner`.

- Use pointers to `IRecliner` and `IChair` interfaces instead of pointers to concrete classes `Recliner` and `Chair_Impl` as data members of `RecliningChair`.

- Use references to interfaces instead of concrete classes as return types for methods in `Recliner`, `Chair_Impl` and `RecliningChair` classes.

7.5.1   The Interfaces

We define an `IRecliner` interface to represent the functions of the reclining mechanism:

```
// File: irecliner.h
// IRecliner class definition
#ifndef IRECLINER_H
#define IRECLINER_H

class IRecliner
{
public:
    virtual void setAngle(int anAngle) = 0;
    virtual int angle() = 0;
    virtual void reset() = 0;
};
#endif
```

We also define an `IRecline` interface to specify the class interface for the reclining function:

```
// File: irecline.h
// IRecliner class definition
#ifndef IRECLINE_H
#define IRECLINE_H

class IRecline
{
public:
```

```
    virtual void setRecline(int anAngle) = 0; // recline seatback
    virtual int recline() = 0;               // get recline angle
};
#endif
```

We define an IChair interface to specify the class interface for a chair:

```
// file: ichair.h
// IChair interface definition
#ifndef ICHAIR_H
#define ICHAIR_H

#include "ChairProperties.h"

class IChair
{
public:
    // methods
    virtual double  sit(double weightOfPerson) = 0;
    virtual double  getOff() = 0;
    virtual double  addWeight(double aWeight) = 0;
    virtual double  removeWeight(double aWeight) = 0;
    virtual double  currentWeight() const = 0;
    virtual bool isBroken() const = 0;
    virtual bool isSitting() const = 0  // true if seated
    virtual void clear() = 0;        // remove load from chair
    virtual void refurbish() = 0;   // make the chair new again!

    // accessor functions for private data members
    virtual ChairProperties::colors color() const = 0;
    virtual IChair& setColor(ChairProperties::colors aColor) = 0;
    virtual ChairProperties::styles style() const = 0;
    virtual IChair& setStyle(ChairProperties::styles aStyle) = 0;
    virtual double capacity() const = 0;
    virtual IChair& setCapacity(double limit) = 0;
};
#endif// file: ichair.h
```

Note that the return type for accessor functions is a reference to IChair interface instead of a concrete class.

These three interfaces are used for implementing the concrete classes.

7.5.2 The Concrete Classes

The definition of the `Recliner` class is changed to use the `IRecliner` interface:

```
// File: recliner.h - Recliner class definition
//
#ifndef RECLINER_H
#define RECLINER_H

#include "IRecliner.h"

class Recliner : public IRecliner
{
private:
    int seatbackAngle;

public:
    Recliner();
    Recliner(int anAngle);
    virtual ~Recliner();
    virtual void setAngle(int anAngle);
    virtual int angle();
    virtual void reset();
};
#endif
```

The changes are highlighted in bold. All `Recliner` objects can now be used through the `IRecliner` interface. The implementation of the `Recliner` class remains the same as before.

The `Chair_Impl` class is changed to use the `IChair` interface:

```
// file: chair_impl.h
// Chair_Impl class definition
#ifndef CHAIR_IMPL_H
#define CHAIR_IMPL_H

#include "ChairProperties.h"
#include "ichair.h"

class Chair_Impl : public IChair
{

private:        // all data members are made private
    ChairProperties::colors acolor;
    ChairProperties::styles astyle;
```

```
    bool            broken;
    double          currentLoad;
    double          maxWeight;
    double          personWeight;
    double          addedWeight;

protected:
    double          setCurrentWeight();

public:
    // constructors and destructor
    Chair_Impl();
    Chair_Impl(ChairProperties::colors aColor,
               ChairProperties::styles aStyle);
    virtual ~Chair_Impl();          // destructor

    // methods
    virtual double  sit(double weightOfPerson);
    virtual double  getOff();
    virtual double  addWeight(double aWeight);
    virtual double  removeWeight(double aWeight);
    virtual double  currentWeight() const;
    virtual bool isBroken() const;
    virtual bool isSitting() const;     // true if person seated
    virtual void clear();           // remove all load from chair
    virtual void refurbish();       // make the chair new again!

    // accessor functions for private data members
    virtual ChairProperties::colors color() const;
    virtual IChair& setColor(ChairProperties::colors aColor);
    virtual ChairProperties::styles style() const;
    virtual IChair& setStyle(ChairProperties::styles aStyle);
    virtual double capacity() const;
    virtual IChair& setCapacity(double limit);
};
#endif
```

The changes are highlighted in bold. All objects of the `Chair_Impl` class can now be used through the `IChair` interface. The accessor methods have also been changed to return a reference to the `IChair` interface instead of `Chair_Impl`.

The implementation of the `Chair_Impl` class will stay the same except for the three modified accessor functions as shown below:

```
IChair& Chair_Impl::setColor(ChairProperties::colors aColor)
```

```
{
    acolor = aColor;
    return *this;
}

IChair& Chair_Impl::setStyle(ChairProperties::styles aStyle)
{
    astyle = aStyle;
    return *this;
}

IChair& Chair_Impl::setCapacity(double limit)
{
    maxWeight = limit;
    return *this;
}
```

Finally, the ReclingChair class definition is changed to use the IChair and IRecline interfaces as shown below:

```
// file: recliningchair.h
// ReclingChair class definition
#ifndef RECLINING_CHAIR_H
#define RECLINING_CHAIR_H

#include "IChair.h"
#include "IRecline.h"
#include "IRecliner.h"
#include <memory>

class RecliningChair : public IChair,
                       public IRecline
{
private:
    // data members use pointers to interfaces instead of
    // pointers to objects of concrete classes
    std::unique_ptr<IChair> chairImpl;
    std::unique_ptr<IRecliner> aRecliner;

public:
    // constructors and destructor
    RecliningChair();
    RecliningChair(ChairProperties::colors aColor,
                   ChairProperties::styles aStyle);
    RecliningChair(RecliningChair &aChair); // copy constructor
```

```
    virtual ~RecliningChair();                // destructor

    // IChair methods
    virtual double  sit(double weightOfPerson);
    virtual double  getOff();
    virtual double  addWeight(double aWeight);
    virtual double  removeWeight(double aWeight);
    virtual double  currentWeight() const;
    virtual bool    isBroken() const;
    virtual bool    isSitting() const; // true if person seated
    virtual void    clear();        // remove all load from chair
    virtual void    refurbish();    // make the chair new again!

    virtual ChairProperties::colors color() const;
    virtual IChair& setColor(ChairProperties::colors aColor);
    virtual ChairProperties::styles style() const;
    virtual IChair& setStyle(ChairProperties::styles aStyle);
    virtual double capacity() const;
    virtual IChair& setCapacity(double limit);

        // IRecline methods
    virtual void setRecline(int anAngle); // recline the seatback
    virtual int recline();                // get recline angle
};
#endif// file: recliningchair.h
```

The changes are highlighted in bold. The `RecliningChair` class uses only the `IChair` and `IRecline` interfaces or C++ built-in data types. No concrete classes are used.

The implementation of the `RecliningChair` class is the same as before. Data members `chairImpl` and `aRecliner`, both pointers to interfaces, are initialized in the constructor to point to objects of concrete classes `ChairImpl` and `Recliner`, respectively. The concrete objects are, however, used through their respective interfaces.

```
RecliningChair::RecliningChair(ChairProperties::colors aColor,
ChairProperties::styles aStyle)
{
    // assign concrete objects to interface pointers
    chairImpl = std::unique_ptr<IChair>
                    (new Chair_Impl(aColor, aStyle));
    aRecliner = std::unique_ptr<IRecliner>(new Recliner());
}
```

The remaining methods of the `RecliningChair` class stay the same. However, we should note that function forwarding to the methods of the `Chair_Impl` class is now implemented using the methods of the `IChair` interface.

7.5.3 Using Interfaces

All `RecliningChair` objects can be used through `IChair` and `IRecline` interfaces as shown in the `main` function below:

```cpp
// Ch07_UsingInterfaces.cpp
//

#include "stdafx.h"
#include "recliningchair.h"
#include <cstdlib>
#include <iostream>

// Generic function using interfaces
void showChairDetails(IChair& aChair, IRecline& aRecline)
{
    aChair.sit(50.0);          // person of weight 50 sits on chair
    aChair.addWeight(25.0);    // add 25 additional weight
    aRecline.setRecline(20);   // recline seatbak 20 deg
    std::cout << std::endl << "Properties of Chair:"
            << std::endl
            << "Weight : " << aChair.currentWeight()
            << std::endl
            << "Color : " << (int)aChair.color() << std::endl
            << "Style : " << (int)aChair.style()
            << std::endl
            << "Recline : " << aRecline.recline()
            << std::endl << std::endl;
}


int main()
{
    // Create a RecliningChair object
    RecliningChair aRecliningChair(ChairProperties::colors::red,
                        ChairProperties::styles::traditional);

    // access RecliningChair methods through
    // IChair and IRecline interfaces
```

```
        showChairDetails(aRecliningChair, aRecliningChair);


        // access RecliningChair methods through the object
        aRecliningChair.sit(150.0);  // the chair will break
        aRecliningChair.refurbish(); // make the chair new again
        aRecliningChair.setColor(ChairProperties::colors::green)
                    .setStyle(ChairProperties::styles::modern)
                    .clear();

    std::cout << std::endl << "Properties of Chair:"
            << std::endl
            << "Weight : " << aRecliningChair.currentWeight()
            << std::endl
            << "Color : "  << (int)aRecliningChair.color()
            << std::endl
            << "Style : "  << (int)aRecliningChair.style()
            << std::endl
            << "Recline : " << aRecliningChair.recline()
            << std::endl    << std::endl;

        return EXIT_SUCCESS;
    }
```

We can write generic code to process objects using interfaces as shown in the function showChairDetails() above. This function can be called by passing as arguments objects of any classes derived from IChair and IRecline interfaces.

7.6   Interfaces and Inheritance

We can also use Interface Base Classes as public virtual base classes to provide a class interface and concrete classes as private base classes to provide implementation. We will do the following:

1. Change the RecliningChair class to inherit its public interface from IChair and IRecline interfaces as public virtual base classes.

2. Declare and implement the methods of the IRecline interface are in the RecliningChair class.

3. We do not explicitly declare or implement the methods of the IChair interface in the RecliningChair class. Instead, we inherit the implementation of IChair interface methods from Chair_Impl by using it as a private base class.

4. Because both `RecliningChair` and `Chair_Impl` classes use the `IChair` interface as a base class, we have to declare the `IChair` interface as a virtual base class of `Chair_Impl`.

5. The `IRecliner` interface methods for the reclining mechanism are inherited from `Recliner` class by using it as a private base class.

The modified `Chair_Impl` class using `IChair` interface as a virtual base class:

```cpp
class Chair_Impl : public virtual IChair
{
  // everything else same as before
}
```

The modified `RecliningChair` class is as follows:

```cpp
// file: recliningchair.h
// RecliningChair class definition
#ifndef RECLINING_CHAIR_H
#define RECLINING_CHAIR_H

#include "IChair.h"
#include "Chair_Impl.h"
#include "IRecline.h"
#include "IRecliner.h"
#include "Recliner.h"
#include "ChairProperties.h"
#include <memory>

class RecliningChair : public virtual IChair,
                       public virtual IRecline,
                       private Recliner,
                       private Chair_Impl
{
public:
    // constructors and destructor
    RecliningChair();
    RecliningChair(ChairProperties::colors aColor,
                ChairProperties::styles aStyle);
    ~RecliningChair();          // destructor

    // IRecline interface methods
    void    setRecline(int anAngle);    // recline the seatback
    int     recline();                   // get recline angle

    // Ichair interface methods inherited from Chair_Impl
```

```
        // IRecliner interface methods inherited from Recliner
};
#endif// file: recliningchair.h
```

There are no changes in the implementation of `Chair_Impl` and `Recliner` classes. The implementation of the modified `RecliningChair` class is given below:

```cpp
// file: recliningchair.cpp
// RecliningChair class implementation

#include "stdafx.h"
#include "recliningchair.h"
#include "chair_impl.h"
#include "recliner.h"

#include <cstdlib>
#include <iostream>

RecliningChair::RecliningChair()
    : RecliningChair(ChairProperties::colors::black,
                     ChairProperties::styles::basic)
{
}

RecliningChair::RecliningChair(ChairProperties::colors aColor,
                              ChairProperties::styles aStyle)
            : Recliner(),
              Chair_Impl(aColor, aStyle)
{
}

RecliningChair::~RecliningChair()
{
}

int RecliningChair::recline()
{
    return angle();
}

void RecliningChair::setRecline(int anAngle)
{
    return setAngle(anAngle);
}
```

The solution works as follows:

1. The public class interface of `RecliningChair` class consists of the `IChair` and `IRecline` interfaces.

2. The `IRecline` methods are declared and implemented in the `RecliningChair` class and are, therefore, accessed directly through an instance of the `RecliningChair` class.

3. We did not to explicitly declare individual `IChair` interface methods in the `RecliningChair` class. Therefore, the individual `IChair` methods are not a part of the public class interface.

4. Because of private inheritance, the methods of the `IChair` interface implemented in the `Chair_Impl` class become private members of the `RecliningChair` class. These private `Chair_Impl` methods cannot be accessed directly through an instance of the `RecliningChair` class.

5. The public abstract methods of the `IChair` public virtual base class in `RecliningChair` automatically delegate to the matching private `IChair` methods inherited from the `Chair_Impl` class. The private `Chair_Impl` methods are, therefore, accessible only by using an instance of the `RecliningChair` class through an `IChair` pointer or reference.

6. The methods of the `Recliner` class become private members of the `RecliningChair` class. We do not make these methods a part of the class interface because they are only used internally by the methods of the `IRecline` interface.

The new `RecliningChair` class is used as shown in the `main` function below:

```
// Ch07_PrivateInheritance.cpp
//
#include "stdafx.h"
#include "recliningchair.h"
#include <cstdlib>
#include <iostream>

int main()
{
    RecliningChair aChair(ChairProperties::colors::red,
                    ChairProperties::styles::traditional);

    // Inherited private methods not accessible through object
    // aChair.sit(50.0);  // does not compile
                        // method not accessible

    // Inherited private methods accessed through IChair*
```

```
    IChair* paChair = &aChair;
    paChair->sit(50.0);    // person of weight 50 sits on chair
    paChair->addWeight(25.0); // add 25 additional weight

    // IRecline interface methods accessed through the object
    aChair.setRecline(20);    // recline seatbak 20 deg

    std::cout << std::endl << "Properties of aChair:"
            << std::endl
            << "Weight : " << paChair->currentWeight()
            << std::endl
            << "Color : " << (int)paChair->color() << std::endl
            << "Style : " << (int)paChair->style()
            << std::endl
            << "Recline : " << aChair.recline()
            << std::endl << std::endl;

    return EXIT_SUCCESS;
}
```

The `IChair` methods of `RecliningChair` are accessed through an `IChair*` while the `IRecline` methods are accessed using the `RecliningChair` object itself. This dual way of using the class interface methods is confusing.

To access the `IChair` methods using a `RecliningChair` object, we have to change the access level of the inherited private methods to public by using *access declarations*. The access declarations declare the names of the private `Chair_Impl` methods in the **public** access control section of the `RecliningChair` class to change their access level from **private** to **public**. The change of access level is possible only for those methods which were public in the `Chair_Impl` base class but became private in the `RecliningChair` class because of private inheritance. Therefore, all `IChair` interface methods implemented in `Chair_Impl` can be made public.

The definition of `RecliningChair` class with access declarations is given below:

```
// file: recliningchair.h
// RecliningChair class definition
#ifndef RECLINING_CHAIR_H
#define RECLINING_CHAIR_H

#include "IChair.h"
#include "Chair_Impl.h"
#include "IRecline.h"
```

```
#include "IRecliner.h"
#include "Recliner.h"
#include "ChairProperties.h"
#include <memory>

class RecliningChair : public virtual IChair,
                       public virtual IRecline,
                       private Recliner,
                       private Chair_Impl
{
public:
    // constructors and destructor
    RecliningChair();
    RecliningChair(ChairProperties::colors aColor,
                   ChairProperties::styles aStyle);
    virtual ~RecliningChair();              // destructor

    // IRecline interface (not a part of Chair_Impl)
    void virtual setRecline(int anAngle);  // recline seatback
    int virtual recline();                 // get recline angle

    // access declaration to restore public access for
    // Chair_Impl methods so that they can also be called using
    // a RecliningChair object
    Chair_Impl::sit;
    Chair_Impl::getOff;
    Chair_Impl::addWeight;
    Chair_Impl::removeWeight;
    Chair_Impl::currentWeight;
    Chair_Impl::isBroken;
    Chair_Impl::isSitting;     // true if person seated
    Chair_Impl::clear;         // remove all load from chair
    Chair_Impl::refurbish;     // make the chair new again!

    Chair_Impl::color;
    Chair_Impl::setColor;
    Chair_Impl::style;
    Chair_Impl::setStyle;
    Chair_Impl::capacity;
    Chair_Impl::setCapacity;
};
#endif// file: recliningchair.h
```

They can now be accessed using a `RecliningChair` object or an `IChair` pointer or reference. The modified main program using this class is given below:

```
// Ch07_PrivateInheritance.cpp
//
#include "stdafx.h"
#include "recliningchair.h"
#include <cstdlib>
#include <iostream>

int main()
{
    RecliningChair aChair(ChairProperties::colors::red,
                          ChairProperties::styles::traditional);

    // inherited private methods accessible through object
    // because of access declaration
    aChair.sit(50.0);        // person of weight 50 sits on chair
    aChair.addWeight(25.0); // add 25 additional weight

    // IRecline interface used through the object
    aChair.setRecline(20);    // recline seatbak 20 deg

    std::cout << std::endl << "Properties of aChair:"
          << std::endl
          << "Weight : " << aChair.currentWeight() << std::endl
          << "Color : " << (int)aChair.color() << std::endl
          << "Style : " << (int)aChair.style() << std::endl
          << "Recline : " << aChair.recline()
          << std::endl << std::endl;

    return EXIT_SUCCESS;
}
```

Using private inheritance in this way hides the implementation details without having to write forwarding functions.

7.7   Guidelines for Class Design

The following guidelines are suggested for designing and using classes:

1. Separate class interface and implementation. Use function forwarding or private inheritance with access declarations to hide implementation details.

2. Use virtual methods in the class interface unless there is a specific reason not to. This avoids confusion caused by hiding of non-virtual methods when using public inheritance.

3. Write as much code as possible using Interfaces. All public methods of a class are potential candidates for creating an Interface. This establishes a *"is usable as"* relationship between the derived class and the Interface.

4. Prefer composition over inheritance.

5. Use public inheritance only to establish an *"is a"* relationship between a derived class and its base class. This is required when a derived class object has to be used through a base class object.

6. When using inheritance, use Interfaces as public virtual base classes to provide a class interface and concrete classes as private base classes to provide implementation.

8   Operator Overloading

An operator in C++ is a function with a name that includes the keyword **operator** followed by the operator being overridden. C++ operators may be overloaded for user defined classes.

8.1   Operator Overloading and Conversions

Most C++ operators can be overloaded with the following restrictions:

- You cannot extend the language by adding new operators
- You cannot change the number of operands that an operator requires (the arity of the operator)
- You cannot change the precedence of an operator
- You cannot change the associativity of an operator
- You cannot change the way an operator works with built-in types
- You cannot overload the ., .*, ::, and ?: operators

The operators that are overloaded most often are the assignment operator =, the mathematical and comparison operators, and the insertion (<<) and extraction (>>) operators. All overloaded operators except the assignment operator are inherited by derived classes.

An overloaded operator for a user-defined class may be defined as member function or as friend function. Some guidelines for operator overloading are as follows:

- Whenever possible, use constant references as parameters for overloaded operators.
- The return type of an overloaded operator must be an object or a reference to an object of the class for which the operator is being overloaded.
- If the left operand of an operator must be an object of your class, use a member function to define the operator. The =, [], () and -> operators must be defined as member functions.

- If the left operand of an operator must be an object of another class, then a friend function must be used. The << and >> operators must be defined as friend functions.

- When a friend function is used, at least one of the arguments of the function must be an object of the class for which the operator is being overloaded.

8.2   Overloaded Operators Example

We will implement the assignment (=), extraction (<<) and insertion (>>) operators for the MarksList class for which implemented a copy constructor in Chapter 5. The definition of the class including overloaded operators is as follows:

```cpp
class MarksList
{
class MarksList
{
 private:
   short numberOfStudents;
   std::vector<double> marks;          // vector to store marks

 public:
   MarksList(short students = 100);    // constructor
   MarksList(const MarksList &aList);  // copy constructor
   ~MarksList();                       // destructor
   short students() const;
   double getMarks(short studentID) const;

   //overloaded operators
   MarksList& operator= (const MarksList &rhs);
   friend std::ostream& operator<< (std::ostream &os,
                                  const MarksList &aList);
   friend std::istream& operator>> (std::istream &is,
                                  MarksList &aList);
};
```

The implementation of the MarksList class stays the same as before:

```cpp
// File markslist.cpp
// Implementation of class MarksList

#include "stdafx.h"
```

```cpp
#include "markslist.h"
#include <iostream>
#include <cmath>

MarksList::MarksList(short students)
{
    numberOfStudents = students;

    // allocate memory for marks array
    marks.resize(students);

    for (int i = 0; i < marks.size(); ++i)
    {
        marks[i] = rand() % 100 + 1;
    }
}

MarksList::MarksList(const MarksList &aList)
{
    // copy data from aList to this list
    numberOfStudents = aList.students();

    marks.resize(numberOfStudents);
    // copy array from aList into marks
    for (int i = 0; i < marks.size(); ++i)
        marks[i] = aList.getMarks(i);
}

MarksList::~MarksList()
{
}

short MarksList::students() const
{
    return numberOfStudents;
}

double MarksList::getMarks(short studentID) const
{
    return marks[studentID];
}
```

We will now implement the overloaded operators.

8.2.1 The Assignment Operator =

The assignment operator is almost the same as the copy constructor. The only difference is that we check for self-assignment before we copy the values from the source object (rhs) to the current object to prevent assigning an object to itself! This is done by comparing the address of the current object (value of **this** pointer) to the address of the rhs object passed as argument. If they are the same, we are trying to assign the object to itself and we should return from the function without doing anything. The complete code for the assignment operator is as follows:

```
MarksList& MarksList::operator=(const MarksList &rhs)
{
   if(this == &rhs)  // guard against self assignment
   {
     return *this;
   }

    // copy data from rhs to this list
    numberOfStudents = rhs.students();

    marks.resize(numberOfStudents);
    // copy array from rhs into marks
    for (int i = 0; i < marks.size(); ++i)
         marks[i] = rhs.getMarks(i);

return *this;
}
```

If we are dealing with a derived class, always assign values to data members of the base class as follows:

- If the base class has an explicitly defined assignment operator, call the assignment operator of the base class to assign values to base class members as follows:

  `BaseClass::operator = rhs;`

- If the base class does not have an explicitly defined assignment operator, use object slicing to convert the current object into a base class object and assign the assign the rhs value to it as follows:

  `((BaseClass&) *this) = rhs;`

This will ensure that we make a complete deep copy of rhs.

8.2.2   The Insertion Operator <<

The insertion operator << prints a formatted list of the marks and is implemented as follows:

```
std::ostream& operator<<( std::ostream &os,
                          const MarksList &aList)
{
   os << "Marks List" << "\n\n"
      << "Number of Students: "
      << aList.numberOfStudents << "\n\n"
      << "Student ID    Marks" << std::endl;

   os << std::setprecision(2) << std::fixed;
   for(int i=0; i < aList.numberOfStudents; ++i)
      {
       os << std::setw(10) << i+1
          << std::setw(10) << aList.marks[i] << std::endl;
      }
   os << "-----------------------" << std::endl;
   return os;
}
```

Note the use of **const** reference to a MarksList object because the purpose of the insertion operator is to print the contents of the object, not to modify it. As a friend function, the operator has access to all public and non-public members of the MarksList class. Therefore, we provide protection against accidental changes by passing a **const** reference.

8.2.3   The Extraction Operator >>

The extraction operator >> for the MarksList class reads input data from a stream. We will assume that the data to be read is available in the following format:

```
20.0 // marks for students
25.0
15.0
...
```

The >> operator to read marks until the end of file is reached is given below:

```
std::istream& operator>>( std::istream &is, MarksList &aList)
{
```

```
    int i = 0;
    while( !is.eof() )
       {
        is >> aList.marks[i];  // store marks in the array
        is.ignore(std::numeric_limits<std::streamsize>::max(),
                  '\n');
        ++i
       }
    aList.numberOfStudents = i;

    return is;
}
```

Note the use of non-constant reference to a `MarksList` object because the purpose of the operator is to read data from a stream and store it in the object: the contents of the object are changed. As a friend function, the operator has access to all public and non-public members of the `MarksList` class.

8.2.4   Using the Overloaded Operators

The `main` program reads data from a file named `marks.txt` and prints the results in file `markslist.txt`:

```
#include <cstdlib>
#include <iostream>
#include <fstream>
#include <iomanip>
#include "markslist.h"

int main()
{
   std::ifstream inputFile("marks.txt");  // create stream
   MarksList aMarksList;
   inputFile >> aMarksList;        // read data into aMarksList
   inputFile.close();              // close input file

   std::ofstream report("markslist.txt"); // create stream
   report << aMarksList;                   // create markslist
   report.close();                         // close output file

   MarksList copiedList = aMarksList;      // copy constructor
   std::cout << "Copied Marks List:\n\n" << copiedList
             << std::endl;
```

```
    MarksList aList(20);
    std::cout << "List before assignment:\n\n" << aList
            << std::endl;
    aList = copiedList;                    // assignment operator
    std::cout << "List after assignment:\n\n"  << aList
            << std::endl;

    return EXIT_SUCCESS;
}
```

If the contents of the file marks.txt are as follows:

```
20.0 // marks for students
25.0
15.0
77.0
56.0
88.0
5.0
```

then the contents of the output file markslist.txt will be as shown below:

```
Marks List

Number of Students: 7

Student ID      Marks
         1      20.00
         2      25.00
         3      15.00
         4      77.00
         5      56.00
         6      88.00
         7       5.00
-----------------------
```

and the output printed on standard output will be as follows:

```
Copied Marks List:

Marks List

Number of Students: 7

Student ID      Marks
         1      20.00
```

```
            2       25.00
            3       15.00
            4       77.00
            5       56.00
            6       88.00
            7        5.00
----------------------

List before assignment:

Marks List

Number of Students: 20

Student ID      Marks
            1       34.00
            2       16.00
            3       40.00
            4       59.00
            5        5.00
            6       31.00
            7       78.00
            8        7.00
            9       74.00
           10       87.00
           11       22.00
           12       46.00
           13       25.00
           14       73.00
           15       71.00
           16       30.00
           17       78.00
           18       74.00
           19       98.00
           20       13.00
----------------------

List after assignment:

Marks List

Number of Students: 7

Student ID      Marks
            1       20.00
```

```
2      25.00
3      15.00
4      77.00
5      56.00
6      88.00
7       5.00
- - - - - - - - - - - - - - - - - - - - -
```

8.3   Overloading Arithmetic Operators

You need to define a set of three functions for every arithmetic operator that is overloaded. The three function are either this set:

```
myClass myClass::operator+(const myClass& rhs) const;
myClass myClass::operator+(long rhs) const;
friend myClass operator+(long lhs, const myClass& rhs);
```

or this set:

```
friend myClass operator+(const myClass& lhs, const myClass& rhs);
friend myClass operator+(const myClass& lhs, long rhs);
friend myClass operator+(long lhs, const myClass& rhs);
```

Operators such as + or * which create temporary objects containing new values must return an object. Operators such as += or *= which modify an existing object can return references to that object using (*this).

The procedure for implementing these operators is similar to the operators implemented in the previous section.

8.4   Class Conversions

There are rules for converting values from one built-in type to another. Sometimes, it is necessary to provide conversions for user defined classes:

- Convert from another user defined class

- Convert from a built-in type

- Convert to another user defined class

- Convert to a built-in type

These conversions are accomplished using constructors and conversion operators.

8.4.1   Convert from Another Type to Your class

Constructors that take only one argument are used as conversion functions. For example, the following constructors will be used to perform implicit conversions as indicated:

```
myClass::myClass(anotherClass& value); // anotherClass to myClass
myClass::myClass(double value);        // double to myClass
myClass::myClass(long value);          // long to myClass
```

If a value of type anotherClass, double, or long is provided where a value of type myClass is required, the C++ compiler uses the appropriate single-argument constructor to convert the value provided to a myClass object.

8.4.2   Convert Your class to Another Type

Implicit conversions from myClass to other types require conversion operators:

```
myClass::operator anotherClass() const; // myClass to anotherClass
myClass::operator double() const;        // myClass to double
myClass::operator long() const;          // myClass to long
```

The conversion operators take no arguments and have no return type. You should never define a conversion operator to int values because it will cause ambiguities that the compiler cannot resolve.

8.4.3   Ambiguous Conversions

If the compiler can interpret a statement in several different ways because of implicit conversions, an error will be generated. For example, the statements

```
myClass a, b;
a = b + 1234;
```

will generate an error because it can be interpreted in two ways:

```
// is it this
a = (long)b + 1234;  // convert b to long using operator

// or this
a = b + (myClLass)1234; // convert long to myClass using
constructor
```

Implicit conversions should, therefore, be used with care.

9   Handling Errors

Our programs may encounter errors during execution. Errors are primarily either logical errors or runtime errors. Our code must make provisions to detect and, if possible, correct errors when they happen and resume execution of the program.

Errors may be handled by having a function returns an error code if an anticipated error occurs. Simple errors, such as a user entering incorrect input, can easily and clearly be handled by checking the input for validity and by requesting the user to input again if the original input is incorrect. However, there are several limitations with this informal approach:

- The code developer can always choose to ignore the error codes returned by a function and let the program continue.

- There will be situations when unanticipated errors happen. They will not be reported.

- There may not be enough information available at the location of the error to recover from the error.

- The error handling code is tightly coupled up with the application logic.

Exceptions in C++ provide a robust error handling capability:

- It provides a mechanism to pass the error information to a location (context) in our program where the error can be handled and the program can recover from the error.

- Exceptions allow the separation of error handling code from the rest of the application logic, making the code easier to understand and maintain.

- Exception cannot be ignored. They have to be handled or the program will terminate.

The use of exceptions require a change in the structure of application programs that depend on function return values for error handling.

9.1   Exceptions

Requires header file `<exception>`.

Exceptions provide a mechanism for a function to notify its caller when it encounters an error it cannot recover from. The notification process is called *throwing an exception*. The point in program execution where the exception occurs is called the *throw point*. The *throw expression* generally throws an object of a class designed explicitly for exception handling. The object thrown is used to transfer error related information from the throw point to the point where the exception is handled (the *exception handler*). C++ implements the termination model of exception handling: when an exception is thrown, control does not return to the throw point.

The caller of a function that throws an exception has the option of "*catching*" and "*handling*" the exception or ignoring the exception and let it go to the next higher level of the program.

9.2   Exception classes

C++ compiler provides several Exception classes all of which are derived from a base class called *std::exception*. We should also use this class to derive our own exceptions classes as follows:

```
#include <exception>

class MyException : public std::exception
{
    virtual const char* what() const throw()
    {
        return "This is my exception";
    }
};
```

The *std::exception* class has a virtual member function called what() that returns a null-terminated string (of type char*) describing the error. We can override this function in our derived exception classes to return a description of the error. The C++ compiler creates a copy of the object being thrown and, therefore, the exception class must have an accessible copy constructor.

9.3   Basic Exception Handling

There are three keywords designed for exception handling in C++: try, catch, and throw.

Statements in a program that might throw an exception are enclosed in braces following the keyword try. This block of statements is called a *try block*.

Immediately following a try block there are one or more blocks of statements preceded by the keyword `catch(catchArgument)` (called *catch blocks* or *exception handlers*). Each catch block identifies the type of thrown objects it can catch in the *catch argument*. We can catch objects, references and pointers of built-in types or objects of any class. A good practice is to catch a `const` reference to the object type being caught. An optional `catch(...)` block may be specified as the last catch block to catch exceptions that have not been caught by other catch blocks. The ellipsis in the catch argument indicates that any type of exception can be handled by this block. However, very limited information is available in `catch(...)` because there is no direct way to access the object thrown.

Try blocks can be nested within other try blocks. You can also nest a try block within a catch block.

```
// code structure for exception handling
...
try
{
  ...
    function1(anArgument); // function1 throws an exception
  ...
}

// std::invalid_argument exception derived from std::exception
catch(std::invalid_argument e)
{
    std::cout << e.what() << std::endl;
}

// std::out_of_range exception derived from std::exception
catch(std::out_of_range e)
{
    std::cout << e.what() << std::endl;
}

// catch std::exception and other classes derived from it
catch(std::exception e)
{
    std::cout << e.what() << std::endl;
}

// optional default catch block rethrows exception
catch(...)
```

```
{
    std::cout << "unknown exception" << std::endl;
        throw;
}
```

When a statement in a try block throws an exception, the remainder of the try block is skipped and search for a matching catch block starts with the catch blocks immediately following the try block containing the throw point. The blocks are searched in order and the control passes to the first catch block whose catch argument matches the type of object thrown based on the following conditions:

- The catch argument type matches the type of the thrown object. For example, the exception handlers for `std::invalid_argument` and `std::out_of_range` exceptions.

- The catch argument is a public base class of the thrown object. However, the thrown object is sliced as it is passed to the handler. Always place a catch block that catches a derived class before a catch block that catches the base class of that derived class. For example, the exception handler for `std::exception`.

- The catch argument specifies a pointer type, and the thrown object is a pointer type that can be converted to the pointer type of the catch argument by standard pointer conversion.

- If no matches are found and a `catch(...)` block exists, the control passes to this block.

- If no matches are found and a `catch(...)` block does not exist, the search ends without finding a match.

During the matching process:

- If the type of the thrown object is `const` or `volatile`, the catch argument must also be a `const` or `volatile` for a match to occur. However, a `const` or `volatile` catch argument can match a non-constant or non-volatile object.

- A non-reference catch argument will match a reference to an object of the same type

Once a match is found, no additional catch blocks are searched. All active code blocks between the throw point and the active catch block are terminated and the destructors are run for all automatic objects constructed in those code blocks. This procedure is called *handling an exception* and the exception is said to be *handled*. The destructor of the thrown object is called after the exception is caught and handled.

When the exception has been handled, the control passes to the first statement after the last catch block in the group. A **return** statement used in a catch block does not return control to the throw point but returns from the function containing the catch block.

If no match is found in the current try block, the search continues in next enclosing try block within the function or the caller of the function that threw the exception. If no matching exception handler is found in the whole program, the exception is declared to be "not handled" and the program is terminated.

9.4   Rethrowing an Exception

When an exception is caught, the information available in the catch block may not be sufficient to recover from the error. In that case, we can process the available information and *rethrow* the original thrown object by using the keyword **throw** without an argument. The **throw** keyword can only be used in a catch block. The rethrow expression causes the originally thrown object to be re-thrown to the next enclosing try block to handle the exception.

9.5   Cleaning Up Resources

Exceptions should be used carefully inside destructors because the control may leave the destructor, resulting in incomplete object cleanup. Resources will not be cleaned properly. If a function that may throw an exception is called in a destructor, it must be contained within a **try** block and an appropriate catch block, usually **catch(...)**, must be provided in the destructor to ensure that the exception does not transfer control outside the destructor.

When an exception is thrown, destructors are called for all automatic objects created since the beginning of the try block from which the exception was thrown. If an exception is thrown during construction of an object composed of other objects (sub-objects) or array elements, destructors will only be called for those sub-objects or array elements that were successfully constructed before the exception was thrown.

Memory allocated using the **new** operator from the beginning of the **try** block up to the throw point has to be deleted explicitly by the exception handlers. This is essential because the control will go outside the **try** block when an exception is thrown and any cleanup code after the throw point will not be executed. This memory management problem can be overcome using C++ smart pointers and containers which have constructors and destructors that handle allocation and de-allocation of memory. The memory will then be freed for objects when their destructors are called by the exception handling mechanism.

9.6 Example: Using Exceptions

The basic use of exceptions is illustrated below:

```cpp
// Ch09_Exceptions.cpp

#include <cstdlib>
#include <iostream>
#include <exception>
#include <string>

// define error class
class DivideError : public std::exception
{
public:
    DivideError(std::string message)
    {
        errorName = message;
    }

    virtual const char* what() const throw()
    {
        return errorName.c_str();
    }

private:
    std::string errorName;
};

// function to perform division
double divide(double a, double b)
{
    // throw exception if b is 0
    if(b == 0)
            throw DevideError("Attempt to divide by zero");
```

```
    return a / b;
}

// the main function
int main()
{
    double a, b, c;

    std::cout << "input numerator: ";
    std::cin >> a;
    std::cout << std::endl << "input denominator: ";
    std::cin >> b;

    try
    {
        c = divide(a, b);
        std::cout << "Result of division is: " << c << std::endl;
    }

    catch (const DivideError& anError)
    {
        std::cout << anError.what() << std::endl;
    }
    catch (...)
    {
        std::cout << "Unknown exception" << std::endl;
            throw;
    }

    return EXIT_SUCCESS;
}
```

The `divide()` function uses the `throw` keyword to throw a `DivideError`
exception which is caught by the caller of the function.

9.7   Exception Specification

C++ provides an *exception specification* for a function to limit the types of
exceptions a function may throw. The exception specification consists of the
keyword `throw` followed by a comma separated list of exceptions enclosed in
parenthesis. An exception specification guarantees that the function will throw only
those exceptions which are listed in the exception specification. However, the C++

compiler does not guarantee that the function will not throw an exception that is not in the list. During execution, a function may actually throw an exception that is not listed in the exception specification. Such an error will be detected only at run time when an unspecified exception is thrown and C++ library function `unexpected()` is called to terminate the program.

A function with an empty exception specification guarantees that the function will not throw any exceptions. A function with no exception specification can throw any exception.

Examples of exception specification are:

```
void function1() throw();     // will not throw any exception
void function2();             // may throw any exception
void function3() throw(exception1, exception2);
```

Function `function1()` cannot throw any exception while `function2()` can throw any type of exception. Function `function3()` can only throw exceptions of type `exception1` or `exception2`.

In general, use of exception specification should be avoided.

9.8   Program Termination

Not all thrown errors can be caught and successfully dealt with by a `catch` block. In some situations, the best way to handle an exception is to terminate the program. Two special library functions are implemented in C++ to process exceptions not properly handled by `catch` blocks or exceptions thrown outside of a valid `try` block: `unexpected()` and `terminate()`. These functions are used by the compiler to terminate the program when the exception handling mechanism fails. By default, `unexpected()` calls `terminate()` and `terminate()` calls the C library function `abort()` to exit from the program. The functions are invoked when:

- When no `catch` block can be matched to a thrown object
- When the stack becomes corrupted during the exception handling process
- When `terminate()` is called explicitly
- When a system defined `unexpected()` is called explicitly

You can write your own termination functions.

- When `unexpected()` is called, it calls the function most recently supplied as an argument to the function `set_unexpected()` instead of calling `terminate()`.

- When `terminate()` is called, it calls the function most recently supplied as an argument to the function `set_terminate()` instead of calling `abort()`. The final action of your function should be to exit from the program. If you attempt to `return` from your function, `abort()` will be called and the program will end.

These set functions are declared in the header files `unexpect.h` and `terminat.h`:

- The argument for both set functions is a pointer to a function that has a `void` return type and does not take any arguments.

- Both set functions return a pointer to the function that was previously called by them. By saving the return values, you can restore the original functions later.

9.9   Guidelines for Using Exceptions

Use exceptions to:

- Transfer error handling to a context where sufficient information is available to handle the error. Try to recover from an exception only if a sensible action can be taken. If the recovery action is not known or obvious, it is better just to report the error.

- Gracefully terminate a program.

- Produce a result that is different from the normal result of calling a function.

- Report errors in constructors.

Some guidelines for using exceptions:

- Never use exception specifications.

- Define a hierarchy of exception classes to handle exceptions of different severity. The base class should formalize a uniform way to catch and recover from errors. Define derived classes only for special cases that will take different recovery actions.

- Use `const` references as catch arguments to prevent problem of object slicing

- Separate error recovery handlers from the resource cleanup handlers. The error recovery handlers may be nested inside the resource cleanup handlers, or let the automatic object cleanup mechanism handle resource recovery.

- Do not use exceptions for errors from which the users may not want to recover. Use standard C++ assertions to signal such errors.

10 Bibliography

1. **Smith, D. N.** *Concepts of Object Oriented Programming.* s.l. : McGraw Hill, 1991.

2. **Barton, J. J. and Nackman, L. R.** *Scientific and Engineering C++: An Introduction with Advanced Techniques and Examples.* s.l. : Addison-Wesley, 1994.

3. **Meyers, Scott.** *Effective C++: 50 Specific Ways to Improve your Programs and Designs.* s.l. : Addison-Wesley.

4. **Teale, Steve.** *C++ IOStreams Handbook.* s.l. : Addison-Wesley, 1993.

5. **Eckel, Bruce.** *Thinking in C++: Introduction to Standeard C++.* s.l. : Prentice Hall.

6. **Taligent.** *Taligent's Guide to Designing Programs: Well Mannered Object Oriented Designs in C++.* s.l. : Addison-Wesley, 1994.

7. **Microsoft Corporation.** *Microsoft C/C++ Version 7: C++ Tutorial.* 1992.